BACK OFFICE
AND BEYOND

BACK OFFICE AND BEYOND

A guide to
procedures, settlements and
risk in financial markets

Mervyn J. King

HARRIMAN HOUSE LTD

43 Chapel Street
Petersfield
Hampshire
GU32 3DY
GREAT BRITAIN

Tel: +44 (0)1730 233870
Fax: +44 (0)1730 233880
email: enquiries@global-investor.com
web site: www.global-investor.com

First published in Great Britain in 1999 by Gilmour Drummond Publishing

This second edition published by Harriman House in association with Gilmour
Drummond Publishing in 2003.

Copyright Harriman House Ltd

The right of Mervyn King to be identified as the author of this work has
been asserted by him in accordance with the Copyright, Design and Patents
Act 1988.

ISBN 1 897 59724 X

British Library Cataloguing in Publication Data
A CIP catalogue record for this book can be obtained from the British Library.

Printed and bound in Great Britain by Biddles Ltd, Guildford.

This publication is designed to provide accurate information in regard to
the subject matter covered. It is sold on the understanding that the
publisher is not engaged in rendering legal, accountancy or other
professional advice or services.

No responsibility for loss occasioned to any person or corporate body acting
or refraining to act as a result of reading material in this book can be
accepted by the publisher, by the author, or by the employers of the author.

CONTENTS

|||

8. Risk Management 109

PREFACE

III

Preface to the 1st Edition

Just how much money has been lost owing to misdirected payments, inefficient management of funds, inaccurate processing, fraud, collusion across all instruments, markets and geographical locations? Does the name Orange County mean anything to you? Have you ever heard of Barings and Nick Leeson? Where were you when BCCI went bust?

Was there ever any danger in dealing with a bank which was one of the 50 largest in the world? Then who was it who caught the biggest cold when LTCM's problems arose? Were not UBS and Bankers Trust involved? Of course, just like contracting a terminal illness or being involved in a road/train/plane accident, it will never happen to you. Want to bet?

From Cinderella to belle of the ball, from necessary evil to board favourite, from an ill-defined philosophy to a science - that has been the history of the back office/settlements function. What has brought about this metamorphosis - the size of the markets, technology, fall-out from past errors or flexibility brought about by the arrival of new instruments?

Why *Back Office and Beyond?* - because the original concept of a back office and its duties was the starting point which has now been extended far 'beyond' its original scope and function. The 'beyond' factor entails not just the changed role regarding processing and payment but also presages the additional requirements now for aspects of risk management to be sited within the back office area. Indeed, back office is intrinsically involved at first base; for if all data is not captured accurately in the first instance, there is little chance of the eventual output, in respect of the institution's risk profile, being accurate.

Already plans are having to be made to incorporate the implications of a single currency in Europe, which again will heavily involve the back office functions. Indeed, it could open up further opportunities for an institution to 'steal a march' on its competitors. The later chapters of this book will explore these developments.

Life began with just a few currencies which traded in small volume at almost fixed levels, where foreign exchange equated to trade only. Now, it has evolved to a multi-faceted market where size and speed of movement has opened up a Pandora's box - if not controlled quickly, efficiently and intelligently. Now, the demand is for all the full implications of risk across its broadest interpretation - risk regarding position/counterparty/correlation to other markets, etc, to be assessed and managed.

On the one hand interaction between markets volume has increased, whereas the onus for wide-ranging experience/knowledge in processing (i.e. not front office) has become heavily compartmentalised and reduced to a single figure evaluation - value at risk (VaR).

How did it all begin? Where are we today? What rules are there? How much interpretation is allowed? How many fixed reference points are there? Had it been left solely to the central banks to cover each variation, then little would probably have been achieved. We only have to look at their inaction at the time of the oil price rises in the 1970s, and the resulting fall-out in the market when commercial loans to emerging countries were not repaid, or the Plaza Agreement and Louvre Accord over-reactions, to judge their contribution. However, there is no real point in citing the problems created by government or their agents when, at the end of the day, timely, accurate and efficient settlement of all trades is the overall goal.

Purpose of this book

Since there is no fixed one-and-only way in which trades can be settled, the purpose of this book is to establish, where possible, those few fixed reference points and what is generally accepted as 'best practice' whilst also identifying some 'caveats' of the pitfalls to look out for, using actual historical events and practical examples.

Despite considerable polarisation of market roles over the last three to five years vis-à-vis the percentage of transactions spread between an ever-decreasing number of principals, every institution still needs to be able to settle its own trades. Thus, whatever their position in the batting order - for example, as identified annually by Euromoney - there is a prerequisite for all transactions initiated by front office to be processed by back office without any loss of income - apart from those accepted as shared universally between departments for funding of accounts and ancillary charges.

Changes in the front office have produced exponential changes in the responsibility level of back office though, via specialisation, the demands for speedy settlement have resulted in fragmentation of responsibility, knowledge and authority with little understanding of respective roles. Pressure can restrict progress! TRAX on bond settlements (see page 45) requires a trade to be entered within 30 minutes of execution; transaction automatic matching systems via the automated time out management system (ATOM/SWIFT Accord /Comfort function (see Appendix 3) imposes time-outs for unreconciled items; individual currency cut-off times make their own demands. With so many banks offering the same products at similar pricing (more and more relevant as the market consolidates/contracts) this means that the one thing that distinguishes one bank from another is the level and quality of service provided to its customers and other banks.

The move to control risk via netting implies simultaneous release of net amounts receivable/payable but does not actually demand it, and VaR figures can only be produced once back office has input all transactions.

How does this all occur? I have naturally approached this exercise from a UK point of view since the UK, London and the Bank of England have been in the forefront of most developments, whether from the front or back office perspective, and remain so today and will be for the future the prime source for 'best practice'.

Market ethics and codes of behaviour have always been better than average in London and it is well known that London's practices are constantly being emulated in the rest of the world, even to the extent that the regular updates of the European Monetary Union (EMU) from the Bank of England are acknowledged as the most professional and thorough and an example to all those central banks which will actually form the core of the first wave of members in 1999.

Obviously, every centre's regulatory set-up has its own local flavour,, but the basics that have been identified for this book will not vary significantly from the UK base. Read on ......

Preface to the 2nd edition

The second edition updates changes that have already occurred since publication of the original edition and anticipates future changes that will affect any settlements/back office/operations department.

Additionally the Repo section has been expanded and - in view of the debacle at Allfirst Bank in the USA - the Risk section has been expanded to give some practical guidance on how to avoid repeating their mistakes. (pp 89 et seq)

Rationalisation/merger activity between banks has meant that institutions need to ensure that their (remaining) staff are fully conversant with all changes and new demands and able to make use of every new advance in mechanisation (= computerisation).

Then due account has to be made of incorporating new systems (web-based trading/single platform delivery etc.) into the current reporting requirements/legislation. You can never afford to take your eye off the ball . .

What has actually occurred?

The basics of the first edition remain as valid as ever, but some things need amending - the Euro is upon us (everyone should now be perfectly conversant with making settlement in that new Euro - even the UK!); a Model Code recommending 'best practice' has been produced and accepted. Other changes have already been signalled - the change to T+1 settlement on bonds (now postponed) and - more significantly -the implications of CAD II, with its capital requirements (due for implementation by 2004) on operational activities are already under active consideration.

The former has not been adopted but not abandoned, just postponed.

On top of that, we are all experiencing the effect of multi-bank portals - Atriax/Currenex and previously (but now defunct) FXAll - offering clients direct access to pricing/confirmation production/audit trails. These bring their own problems to the operations area re integration with other systems and the in-house accounting.

Additionally, albeit very briefly, this edition looks at the settlement function in relation to equities. It is not be an in-depth study, as that would require a complete tome in its own right, given the variation in operation, trading and settlement between various major exchanges. Since, however, the author believes equity trading is likely to become a more important area in revenue, it was thought worthwhile to include a basic guide.

Enough of these generalisations .. let's on to the fray!

CHAPTER 1

▌▌▌

IN THE BEGINNING ...

One of the many concerns arising from the advances in information technology, financial innovation, deregulation and intensified competition has been the vast growth in the volume and value of financial transactions across the world's payments and settlements systems. (See Bank for International Settlement (BIS) survey results on page 140. In the UK alone, some £120 billion of settlements occur daily of which about half is constituted by the sterling settlement of foreign exchange transactions. Additionally about the same amount (£120 billion) is settled daily representing money market, gilt-edged and equity payments. If one extrapolates the figure for global operations, then in foreign exchange alone some $2 trillion exchange hands each day.

It will easily be appreciated therefore that as these numbers have increased there has been a commensurate increase in the payment and settlement risk implicit within them. The risk that, after having settled - or at least sent the payment instructions - the sold/lending side of the transaction or the receivable amount due is either received late or not at all.

Every bank/institution relies upon the receipt of funds in order to be confident of being able to honour other commitments. Any payments/settlement failure could have very serious consequences upon the whole payments system - not just in the local currency but on a global scale. Such a catastrophe would be capable of creating a complete 'gridlock' (known as '**systemic risk**') on the global payments system - given the degree of interdependence - with a resultant inestimable effect upon trust/credit worthiness.

Obviously, there have been changes, which in most cases are consistent with improvements but, although the ultimate funds transfer may be handled via computers, the instructions are generated by a human being who is fallible. Thus the efficiency and reliability of the back office staff and their appreciation of the risks of the operations of the front office is paramount. Similarly, the attention given to training in this vital area and its ability to keep up with the developments of both instruments and systems, will single out some institutions from others as the preferred trading partners of counterparties. Furthermore, as further rationalisation takes place in both the number of institutions being actively involved in the financial markets and the instruments traded have less liquidity, the back office could assume even greater importance, as institutions vie for the available business.

The list of 'near misses' and general concern regarding the size and impact of mistakes and fraud on the vast sums involved has led to central banks being involved in encouraging banks and computer companies to come out with new/efficient controls and in establishing some of their own recommendations on minimum acceptable levels of control. As ever, however, the onus for action has remained with the commercial banks.

History

Although history does seem to repeat itself, it is not the purpose of this book to trace the history of front office/back office relationships beyond 1946.

Why 1946? At that point the United States dollar (USD) was established as the numeraire for world trade and became the currency in which most transactions were expressed, commodities were priced and reserves were held (see Tables 1.1 and 1.2).

Given that the USD was replacing the now less relevant, and economically fraught, Great Britain pound (GBP), the major currency in which transactions took place was GBP/USD - known as 'cable' - as the price in those days was transmitted via the cable that went under the Atlantic Ocean. At this stage, however, the size of trade was small (still recovering after the Second World War) and thus individual transaction size, the spread in the price, and the speed of delivery were all extremely different to those of today.

Table 1.1 - World's reserves by currency -$bn (source:IMF)

	Total	USD	EUR	JPY	GBP	CHF
1999 Q1	1,597.6	1,019.3	201.0	80.4	59.6	10.3
1999 Q2	1,636.9	1,054.8	196.0	77.6	61.3	10.3
1999 Q3	1,705.7	1,090.2	207.1	86.8	64.1	10.5
1999 Q4	1,773.8	1,133.6	209.0	91.0	65.8	10.7
2000 Q1	1,799.2	1,153.8	214.6	93.8	67.1	11.5
2000 Q2	1,849.6	1,185.7	217.6	92.2	66.9	11.8
2000 Q3	1,869.3	1,290.6	213.6	93.7	67.3	11.7

In percentage terms over the period, the USD increased its share from 64% to 69%; EUR decreased from 12.5% to 11.4%; JPY stayed stable at 5%; GBP declined marginally from 3.7% to 3.6% and the CHF stayed around 0.6%.

The effects of the depredations of the war, the size of world trade at that time and the less exiguous demands regarding settlement were not the only influencing factors. At that stage, the actual number of currencies that were tradeable was far smaller, as were the number of active trading centres and principals involved - there were i.e. no huge flows from mutual funds (Soros/Paul Tudor, etc.) or cross-boundary investment in bonds or stocks. Also, the state of technology had a lever effect on the status, relevance and efficiency of any so-called 'settlement' function.

What has been experienced since that time, the market has evolved in stages:

• Simple foreign exchange (FX) and money market (MM)

      Spot and forward up to one year
      Fixed deposits

• More currencies/instruments

      Forward up to five years
      Capital market instruments

Table 1.2 Official Foreign Exchange Reserves by Region
(sources: IMF; national data; BIS estimates)

Changes at current exchange rates

	1997	1998	1999	2000	Outstanding at end 2000
Total	56.1	55.9	129.6	139.5	1,908.7
Industrial countries	-12.0	-11.3	40.7	54.5	774.8
Asia [1]	8.5	62.2	79.1	46.4	688.4
Latin America [2]	10.9	-8.3	08.0	2.4	127.6
Eastern Europe [3]	4.9	5.1	0.6	21.2	95.2
Other countries	43.8	8.2	17.2	15.0	227.0

[1] China, Hong Kong, India, Indonesia, Korea, Malaysia, the Philippines, Singapore, Taiwan and Thailand.

[2] Argentina, Brazil, Chile, Colombia, Mexico and Venezuela

[3] Bulgaria, Croatia, the Czech Republic, Estonia, Hungary, Latvia, Lithuania, Poland, Romania, Russia, Slovakia and Slovenia.

Changes, at constant exchange rates
partly estimated; valued at end-of-year exchange rates

	1997	1998	1999	2000	Outstanding at end 2000
Total	113.5	18.6	181.0	172.1	1,908.7
Dollar reserves	72.5	51.3	140.3	130.3	1,450.5
Non-dollar reserves	41.0	-32.7	40.7	41.8	458.2

• Off balance sheet/derivative markets
> FRAs
> Futures
> Swaps
> Options

All through this period of development, central banks have become more and more concerned about the operations/risks of the markets and thus become more demanding as to the reports that they receive. Their real concern has been the fear of 'systemic' risk or 'gridlock' referred to earlier - i.e. the chance of the whole market coming to a standstill because of the failure of a major player in one or other market.

Systemic risk

The problems of the Long Term Capital Management (LTCM) fund could have been 1998's offering for a systemic failure. In this case it was a non-bank where concern over the lack of control compared to that imposed on banks has often been expressed. However, the impact was upon the banking system and could have had disastrous, domino effects.

The Federal Reserve organised a $5.9 billion bail-out when it saw a 50% chance that the whole US financial system might unravel. The Fed was not so much concerned with the investors who would lose several billion dollars, but with the risk that several credit and interest rate markets would experience extreme price movements and cause markets to close temporarily. This, in turn, could then have led to a general loss of investor confidence, the widening of credit spreads, more liquidations of positions and then to an interested cost of capital to American business.

LTCM lost over 50% of its capital through a misjudgement of emerging markets in which it had leveraged itself via derivative instruments up to an exposure of $100 billion. Fourteen institutions were brought together by the Fed to bail out LTCM - including some banks who had additional exposure via direct investment in LTCM.

While such an eventuality is not entirely preventable, it could have been mitigated had the requirements of reporting and management of risk, which are now in force, been in place then.

Self-regulation has been tried to back up internal controls, but lapses still occur. It is, however, more far-reaching in the financial world (i.e. banking) for a number of reasons:

- The central role occupied by banks in the payments system.

- The need for confidence in what is a fragile environment running massive transfer of funds.

- The inextricability of the simultaneous inter-relationship of banks and overlapping instruments with the possibility of systemic collapse (see Fig 1.1).

Fig 1.1 - Close Shaves

(for fuller details of some of these see March 1996 edition of BIS publication, Settlement Risk in FX Transactions, sections 2.2.1 - 2.2.5)

Herstatt	6/74 - Buba closes bank at 10.30 - halfway through day.
Contill	1982/4 - insolvent.
Bank of New York	11/95 - computer failure threat to CHIPS system - $23bn bailout by Federal Reserve Bank.
BCCI	7/91 - liquidated before paying out to UK and Japanese counterparty - fraudulent dealing.
Invasion of Kuwait	8/90 - B of E and other counterparty banks (CBs) avoided gridlock on dinar.
Soviet Coup	8/91 - counterparty banks refused to pay out to Soviet banks, even though they had paid countervalues.
Barings	2/95 - after its collapse, ECU clearing almost gridlocked.

Each of the situations cited in Fig 1.1 has led to a renewed attempt to impose further controls from without, when the original problem stemmed from within - either through lack of internal controls or failure to maintain them. The original Banking Act of 1879 might have been expected to put that right, requiring, as it did, 'every bank which registers under the act to publish at least once per year its exact financial position ... and to submit their books to external auditor's. Such optimism had not anticipated the Bank of Credit & Commerce International (BCCI) scenario (but see new developments under Pillar 3 of CAD II).

The problem with the reliance on auditors to 'do the necessary' ignores the fact that an external auditor, works for, is paid by and has his primary duty to the client, although that is now under review. Other external intervention would have to be so intrusive, pervasive and expensive as to be immediately unenforceable.

As a result the onus, responsibility (and sometimes blame) must rest with the internal controlling departments and the auditor - although there is still room for the central authorities which can calibrate the external burden of regulation by (say) the number of visits, frequency of reporting or the range of products allowed. If one refers back to the Barings case, Barings was understood to have an excellent VaR model in operation, yet it did not enforce that oldest and most vital first control - segregation of back office duties and reporting lines. Technical expertise can never offset or prevent human failings (or fraud).

This vital support role offered by back office has always been seen as a non-profit making area - front office merely depends on it not to lose the profit already made - but, considering the overall scope of the modern settlement function, it should be quite easy to appreciate that the few extra points gained in the price of the trade pale into insignificance when compared to the cost of a failed settlement.

The repercussions could be limited to a small fixed charge for an amendment to the beneficiary or date, via the more serious overdraft charge to the extreme, although not impossible, situation in which a failed settlement was instrumental in a failed share purchase/company take-over/bond issue with resultant bankruptcy a strong possibility.

Enough of the generic, let's look at the specifics!

CHAPTER 2

▌▌▌

THE SET-UP
AND ROLE
OF BACK OFFICE

Set-up

The first essential in every bank is that the dealing function is separated from the settlements function and that both have separate management reporting lines. The set-up incorporates not only the personnel, systems and hardware but also the correct relationship between the staff and duties of front/back /middle office.

A dealer should never have the opportunity to make a payment on a deal and, conversely, settlements staff should never have an opportunity to undertake a market deal or write up a deal ticket. Therefore, the FX/MM dealing environment where the deal is initially concluded must always be separated from the settlements department where payments are made. This so-called 'Chinese Wall' divides the lines of responsibility between the two departments. It follows, therefore, that reporting lines have to be strictly separated, which if not clearly established and monitored (see Fig 2.1), could result in another Barings, Singapore, case - although the new Model Code now allows for one back office to serve more than one front office and for circumstances in which no physical separation is possible.

Co-operation is obviously a *sine qua non* but a good back office will keep on top of the front office and try to anticipate problems and plan accordingly. Mutual appreciation including knowledge of respective roles will make the difference between a growing reputation for your institution (and a participating bonus!) and a major loss of money, reputation and - maybe - your actual job!

Fig 2.1 - Front office/back offfice reporting lines

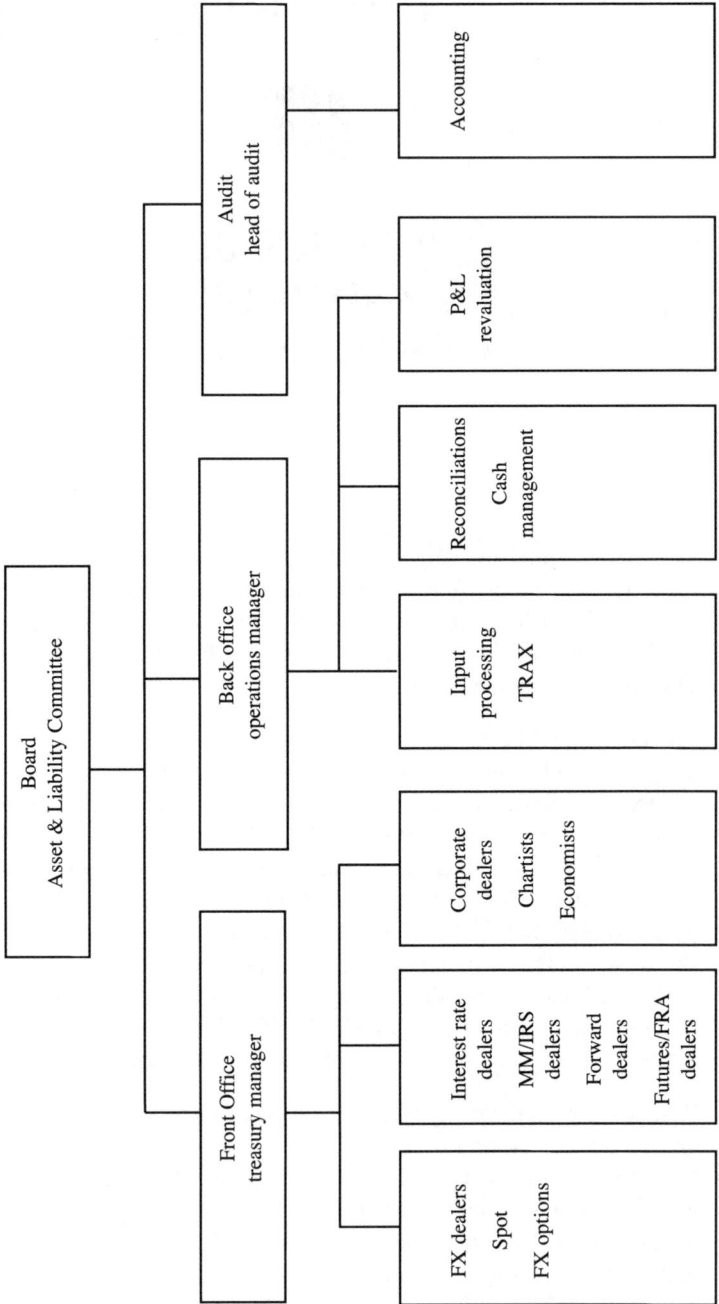

Fig 2.1 - Front office/back offfice reporting lines

Board
Asset & Liability Committee

Front Office
treasury manager

FX dealers
Spot
FX options

Interest rate
dealers
MM/IRS
dealers
Forward
dealers
Futures/FRA
dealers

Corporate
dealers
Chartists
Economists

Back office
operations manager

Input
processing
TRAX

Reconciliations
Cash
management

P&L
revaluation

Audit
head of audit

Accounting

Co-operation without any undue familiarity entails the monitoring of actual family/relationship ties. It is also vital that relations (brothers/sisters, husbands/wives, boyfriends/girlfriends, etc) are not employed in interdependent roles. Thus, management must always be aware of any such relationships to ensure that there is no potential for collusion between a dealer and someone in the back office which could lead to trades being altered, payment instructions changed or revaluation rates being doctored.

Attention to 'system security' will assist in this area. This entails ensuring that only those authorised have access to systems or parts thereof. For example:

- Codes for releasing payments through Society for Worldwide Interbank Financial Telecommunications (SWIFT), Clearstream, Euroclear, etc, should be restricted to those authorised to release such payments.

- Sensitive information (e.g. revaluation rates/programmes) should be either password or 'view only',protected to prevent unauthorised access/tampering.

- All staff with password-protected access should be trained to sign off when away from their terminals.

In the same context, although for a different purpose, back office staff will be responsible for correct retention period for records - i.e. the legal and/or 'recommended' period for retention of records varies both by law and by internal rules according to type. If insufficient attention is given to the set-up then all the roles that flow from it are at risk of failure.

The role of back office

The actual title given to the function will vary between any of the following:

- Back office
- Back-up
- Settlements
- Middle office
- Support

Normally the justification for the specific title describing the role is dependent upon the size and role of the front office. So, whatever it is called (see Fig 2.2), what is/should be the function of this area?

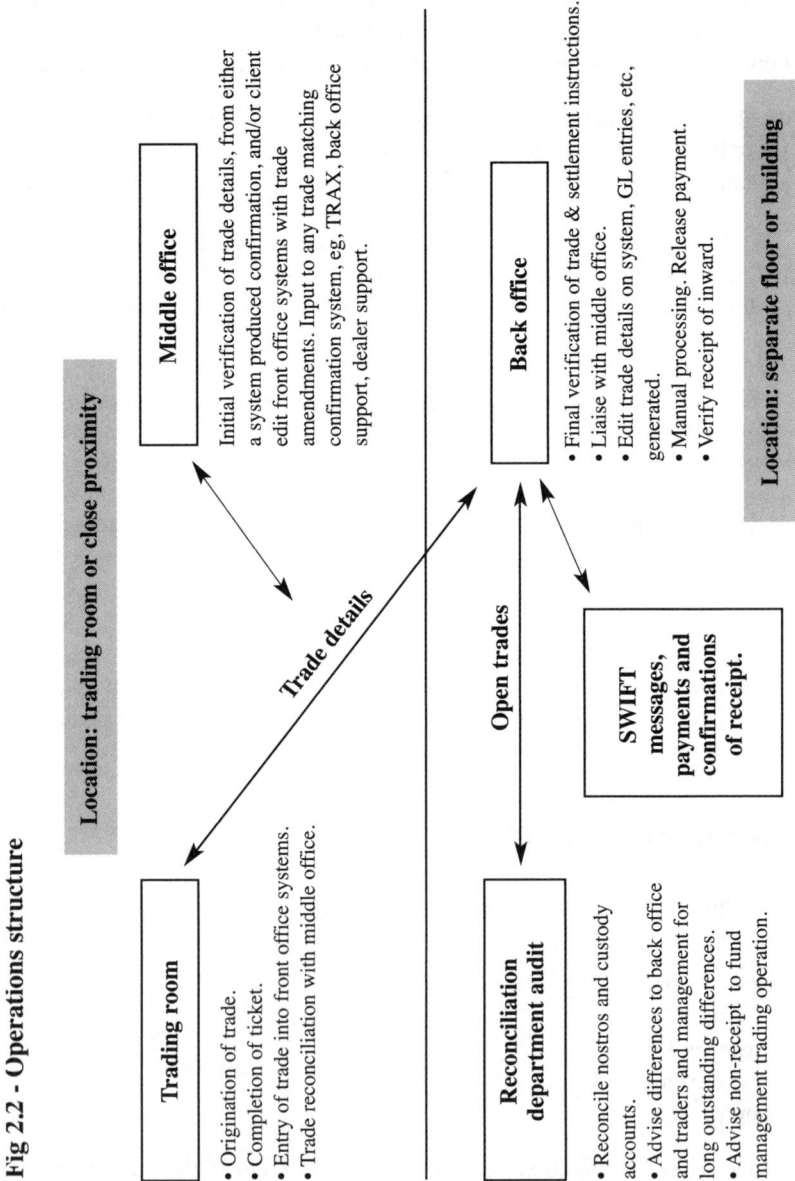

Fig 2.2 - Operations structure

Location: trading room or close proximity

Middle office

Initial verification of trade details, from either a system produced confirmation, and/or client edit front office systems with trade amendments. Input to any trade matching confirmation system, eg, TRAX, back office support, dealer support.

Trading room

- Origination of trade.
- Completion of ticket.
- Entry of trade into front office systems.
- Trade reconciliation with middle office.

Trade details

Back office

- Final verification of trade & settlement instructions.
- Liaise with middle office.
- Edit trade details on system, GL entries, etc, generated.
- Manual processing. Release payment.
- Verify receipt of inward.

Location: separate floor or building

Open trades

SWIFT messages, payments and confirmations of receipt.

Reconciliation department audit

- Reconcile nostros and custody accounts.
- Advise differences to back office and traders and management for long outstanding differences.
- Advise non-receipt to fund management trading operation.

The essential role covers the three main areas of reputation, risk and reward where the market forces which drove them can be summarised as in Fig 2.3., plus the actual settlement and post-settlement functions.

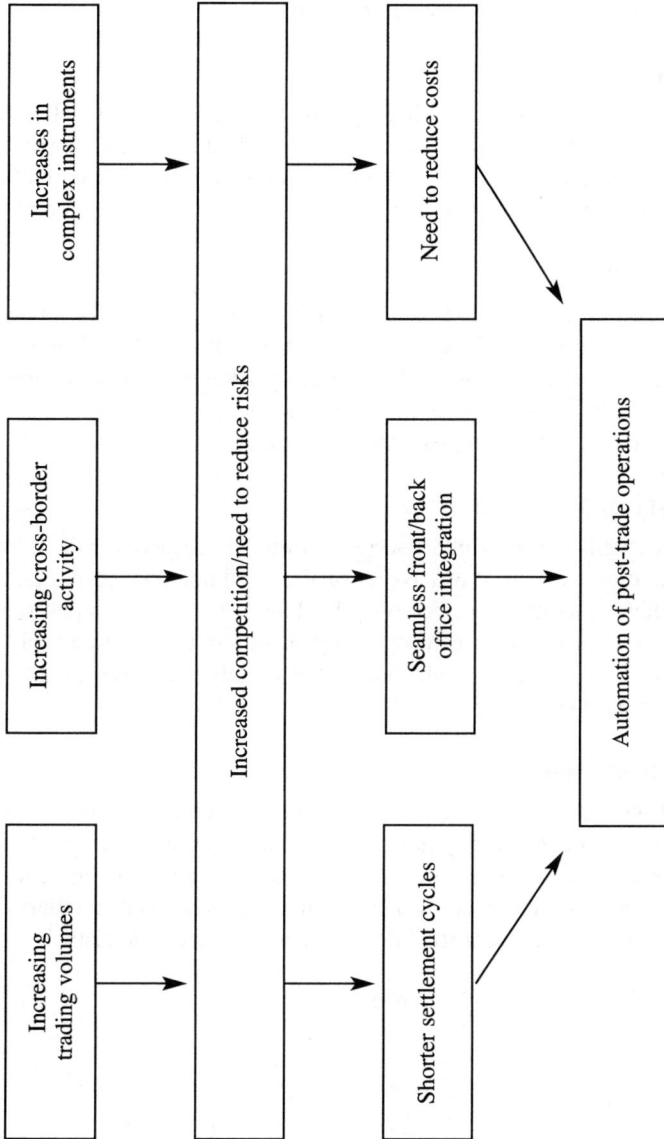

Fig 2.3 - Market forces

Reputation

Any institution needs to protect its reputation in what is a most competitive market. An excellent service from the front office can all too easily be destroyed by an inefficient back office. Thus a courteous, efficient processing and follow-up operation can make all the difference. A reputation lost is not easily regained!

Risk

Risk management is very high profile in today's markets. However, the risk cannot be properly managed if the original input is either incomplete or inaccurate, which then leads to incorrect data being included in management or external reports.

Reward

Back office cannot make money, but it could quite easily dissipate profits earned by the front office. An efficient back office today has the incentive to perform to its utmost by the right to participate in front office profits. Essentially the back office role falls into two phases - physical settlement of all transactions and post-settlement functions.

Physical settlement

This entails carrying out a series of duties in respect of all transactions emanating from front office (treasury, capital markets, corporate finance, syndicated loans, etc) effectively leading to making an actual payment - in full or as part of a netting arrangement - in the right currency, in the right place and at the right time. This sounds easy, doesn't it? What on earth could go wrong?

Post-settlement

This will involve a plethora of responsibilities relating to the consequences of the processing/payment (e.g. confirmations/SSIs and account maintenance) to the consequences (e.g. cash management, nostro reconciliation and margin account management) and ancillary matters (e.g. management reports, P&L calculations, tapes and risk).

Let's now take this step by step.

Processing

From the moment a trade/deal is struck (see Fig 2.4), front office is only thinking of how and when to turn it into a profit. Thereafter, as far as it is concerned, it has completed its involvement with that trade and all subsequent responsibility passes to the back office. Since back office will also handle internal transactions - i.e. transactions between two sections of its own institution - there should be no temptation/excuse to treat such deals any differently from those with external clients. The same degree of control should be exercised whatever the source of the trade.

Fig 2.4 - The FX transaction flow

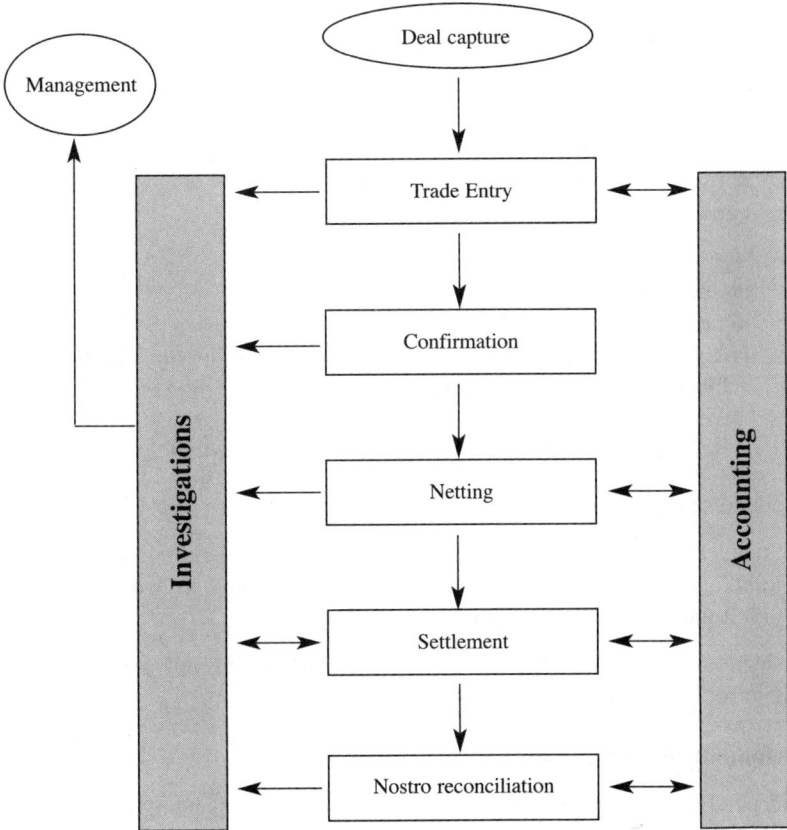

Deal completed by front office

Are the details of the deal complete? Well, what should be included? This depends, once again, on the size, mechanisation, etc., of the front office operation depending on whether the deal tickets are manually completed, partially mechanised or dealt with by straight-through processing.

Basically, the trade should have the following:
- the counterparty (bank or corporate client) with whom the host bank has traded.
- the amount and currency sold (and amount borrowed or loaned if MM deal).
- the amount and currency bought (and interest amount if MM deal).
- the exchange rate of the deal (and interest rate if MM deal).
- the value date of the deal (and maturity date if MM deal).
- the medium through which the deal was made (e.g. broker/phone/Reuters/telex).

Is the deal written for the:
- correct amount?
- correct value date?
- correct counterparty - name and branch?
- correct currency pair?

Are the settlement details:
- included at all?
- in agreement with SSI?
- possible? (You cannot pay Swiss francs (CHF) to the Bank of Tokyo.)
- subject to a netting agreement?

If all is in order, then the deal can be released to the computer, the input can be checked, released to the accounts department, the pay instruction can be sent and confirmation awaited.

Not every one of these details is relevant to every type of transaction, and points such as maturity, settlement amount and settlement method present a multitude of choices and potential confusion.

Thus, these details may be missing, included but not needed, and incorrect anyway.

Manually completed tickets

Depending upon the number of individual input forms being used, some minor or major understanding of the transaction involved is required of the processing staff in order that the deal ticket is both complete and accurate. This could mean something relatively simple, in the case of Spot = 2 currencies and amounts:

- Deal date
- Counterparty
- Value date
- Exchange rate
- Intermediary (phone/European Banking System (EBS)/Reuters 3000/broker/e-commerce/Web portal)

An interest rate swap (IRS) needs all the above plus:

- Day basis for interest calculation.
- Interest payment basis (annual/semi-annual; money market or bond basis).
- Currency of interest payments.
- Documentation - International Swap and Derivative Association (ISDA) / British Banker's Association Interest Rate Swap (BBAIRS) /other.
- Exchange rate (if a currency rate swap - CIRS).
- Settlement medium - Euroclear/Clearstream/Fedwire, etc.

Partially mechanised tickets

This situation occurs when either all EBS or Reuters 3000 deals have 'default' data already supplied or when some data is automatically inserted to the deal typed, for example, an internal system produces its own deal ticket from a blank format on to which all relevant data is transcribed. However, this effectively leaves back office with the need to check/make amendments to all/some deals as in a manual situation.

Straight-through processing

Here, there is no need for intervention by back office in supplying and checking details and the deal passes via computer input system to an automatic confirmation system, to the generation of the payment via the appropriate medium (SWIFT/Clearing House Interbank Payment System (CHIPS)/Clearing House Automated Payment System (CHAPS), CLS etc (see Appendix 3). All that is left is to release the payment - which itself is now very often included in STP at the most active banks.

CHAPTER 3

███

THE LIFE OF A DEAL

Whatever the niche of any institution, and whether the deal is manual, partly mechanised or completed by straight-through processing, the essential elements of a deal follow the following steps.

Deal capture

Originally, the back office would have been responsible for the deal capture of all details as automised/customised front office systems did not exist. Thus, once the dealer had manually entered the basic data, the back office staff would also manually enter all other details. This would have entailed a multitude of individual records for each type of transaction plus the master card, for example:

- Spot CHF purchased
- Spot CHF sold
- Forward CHF purchased
- Forward CHF sold

NCR 32 machines were a favourite semi-mechanised system for this, with huge bins of cards for all the records. End of year reconciliations and then subsequent transfers to computer-based systems were a nightmare! At least at that stage there was not the plethora of instruments or the inter-related position reports required.

The duties, however, were just the same as today - accurate recording, speedy transmission of payments and reconciliation of differences were and remain essential. Any back office worth its salt would insist that its efficiency has never been in doubt, but it is worth bearing in mind that 'prevention is better than cure' - i.e. it is much better to get the initial payment right, for it can be very difficult/time-consuming and costly to get a payment returned.

Front office systems

Some banks develop their own computer systems for capturing and recording the life of a deal. Others purchase proprietary front office systems originally - REMOS or Reuters - today many other partial and complete software solutions are available. In general, the more sophisticated and automated the front office system, the less manual processing and calculating is required (see Appendix 3).

Whatever the system, the component parts are the same. So what are they?

Deal ticket encoding

All banks have a system for encoding new deal tickets. Encoding serves to identify the counterparty with whom the host bank has traded. There are many ways to achieve this, usually a unique number or mnemonic is used which will then display the full name and postal/SWIFT address of the counterparty. This code will often also be used to help to collate data regarding the host bank's exposure to particular counterparties in terms of amounts and also by the industrial sector for corporate clients.

Swapping instructions

Having first been entered into the dealer's front end system, the deal ticket must then be passed electronically or manually to the back office for processing and settlement (i.e. payment of the sold or loaned currency and/or receipt of the purchased currency or repaid loan).

In order to be able to execute such payments, the back office must know or find out the payment instructions of the counterparty. There are several different ways and stages at which a bank can add delivery instructions to a deal ticket and this has to be done in accordance with its internal policy. Some dealers will leave all the settlement instructions to be added by their back office. Some dealers will add instructions to deals with overseas counterparties (or they are added by the automated processing system) but request the back office to add instructions to deals with local counterparties. Some banks endeavour to use SSIs on all or just selected counterparties. It may also be possible that different SSIs are exchanged for different types of operation, for example, a different nostro in the same currency for FX, MM and bond transactions.

Standing settlement instruction (SSI) agreements

An SSI agreement is a legally binding arrangement established between two parties. The objective of the agreement is very simple. Normally, without an SSI agreement, the two parties involved in a trade would have to either exchange delivery instructions via the dealing medium (e.g. broker or Reuters) when the deal is struck if they were in different countries, or exchange instructions by telephone if they were both in the same country.

When two parties sign and commence an SSI agreement, they advise each other at which nostro correspondent they will always take delivery of specified currencies. Therefore, on all future trades, there is no need to advise one another where they receive traded currencies as this has already been established. An SSI agreement is also known as a 'non-swapping agreement' as the two parties involved no longer have to swap instruction on all of their future trades.

Therefore, for example, if Bank A and Bank B enter into an SSI agreement, every time Bank A sells or loans Bank B some Yen, there is no need to swap instructions as Bank A already knows that Bank B always takes delivery of its JPY at say, Mitsubishi-Tokyo, Tokyo.

The use of SSIs is growing each year and some central banks issue guidelines and advice on the best practice which should be used in such agreements - for example, advising the minimum notice period which should be given when one party has changed its nostro correspondent in a particular currency.

SSI agreements are popular because they reduce processing costs and reduce the risks of both error and fraud. Additionally, SSI agreements help facilitate straight-through processing of deals. The Bank of England recommends that SSIs be exchanged by SWIFT and warns strongly against accepting fax instructions. (page. 47-8 of the Model Code)

One possible problem with SSIs is that, since instructions are not sought on a deal-by-deal basis, a deal could be processed and payments sent on a deal which has been incorrectly recorded between two institutions. This would only be possible on deals done over the phone or via a broker between two institutions in the same centre and would normally be discovered before payments are sent, but on short date trades the problem becomes greater. Obtaining the return of funds then can become quite time-consuming and problematical for reconciliation. Automated matching systems would obviously assist here (see Appendix 3). It devolves upon the back office to ensure that all SSI details are monitored, including:

- The original exchange
- Updates
- Schedules for renewals
- Input into internal processing system
- The format of advice, i.e. fax or telephone is not sufficient on its own

An exception to the use of SSIs exists in many banks in London in respect of deals done today for either value today or tomorrow. The rationale for this is that confirmations would possibly not be exchanged in time - even to get matched via a matching system - before payment is due.

Validation of data

The treasury back office is where monetary payments are made and, as such, strict procedures and internal controls are necessary to avoid the risk of unauthorised payments being made and to protect the bank and its customers generally. This is especially relevant in the case of requests for amendments to details - reports to management on details of amended details is a good control. In forward FX swaps, amendments have to be very carefully monitored, for if the first leg has already matured and the swap details are subsequently amended, the true profitability will be affected unless the points differential between the spot and forward leg is maintained.

Each bank will have its own internal controls and policies to ensure the accuracy and validity of deal data and to make sure that each new deal received in the back office from the dealing room is a genuine and *bona fide* transaction. The things to check are that no basic data is missing, a Reuters slip is attached when it should be, etc.

Most computer systems are designed with a series of checks and balances to ensure that the deal ticket received by the back office is valid and accurate. Some banks may also have a policy of ensuring that either a broker or counterparty confirmation is received before the payment on the trade can be released. Other banks check each Reuters dealing slip against each trade prior to executing payment. The variation on the overall theme of the need to validate before making irrevocable release of a payment will relate back to the degree of automation employed in the overall processing operation.

Straight-through processing could be a problem here, but only if the initial set-up was not originally validated. For manual or semi-automated operations, the two major hang-ups could be release against one signature when more than one is required and the lack of authorised signatories at time-sensitive moments (e.g. last cut off for value same day payments).

There are a variety of ways to ensure the integrity of deal data. However, each bank must satisfy itself and usually its local banking regulatory authority that its system is as fraud-proof as possible.

Third party payments

There are situations where the purchaser, borrower or the 'normal' beneficiary of funds may require the paying bank to execute its payment to a beneficiary other than itself. In other words the host bank's counterparty requests that the funds actually due to it be paid to a third party. Whereas in the vast majority of instances, the counterparty requires the payment to be made directly to its own account, the paying bank is executing a third party payment and thus runs the risk of these funds being fraudulently diverted into an unauthorised account.

Every bank takes a number of measures to protect itself from this risk of loss and, indeed, some banks refuse altogether to make third party payments because of the inherent risk. One method that can be used to reduce this particular risk is for banks to insist on receiving special mandates or authorisation from their customers who require such third party payments to be made. Such authorisations from the counterparty to the paying bank would normally state specifically the currencies, the maximum amounts and the individuals employed by the organisation who are authorised to request such payments. The mandate may even specify the actual names of the only third party beneficiaries that may be entertained. Also, there may be other controls in place such as the requirement to phone back a different-named individual at the company to the one who gave the original instruction, or even code words may be used.

Where the special mandates do exist, it is the responsibility of the paying bank to ensure that the customer's and bank's instructions are followed precisely. There remains, of course, the risk of collusion between members of staff employed by the bank, the customer's institution or both. However, each bank must be aware of the dangers and employ appropriate measures and practices to combat the risk of fraud - i.e. carry out effective 'due diligence'.

Releasing confirmations/payments

Because of the ever-present risk of fraud inside financial institutions, all back offices should have a system whereby at least two individuals are required to release trades. This is particularly the case where the actual deal payment is being released. Some bank's systems have the functionality to require a third person to verify the release of a payment, particularly when there is an exceptionally large amount involved, if it is a third party payment or if payment is contingent upon some other event. The goal, however, of straight-through-processing (STP) still makes it hard to control these areas.

Since some correspondents will only action a maximum amount of payments before matching amounts received - so-called daylight exposure limit - it is important that priority payments are released ahead of others and that the current total of payments in progress is monitored to avoid any embarrassment with both the agent and the recipient.

Treatment of exceptions

Where discrepancies arise between the host bank's own record of the deal and the incoming broker or counterparty confirmation, these differences must be advised to the dealing room as quickly as possible. However, it is imperative that control procedures are always adhered to and that contact between the front and back office in such situations is strictly in accordance with established lines of communications. Some banks have a strict policy whereby dealing personnel are not allowed in the back office and only selected back office staff are allowed to enter the dealing room.

A good general rule of thumb is that original incoming confirmations which are unidentified or which have discrepancies should never be left with the dealer who would have struck the trade if it were genuine, but should be presented to the head of section to be referred to the appropriate dealer. However this is not a rule applicable to all banks. Automated matching systems again are relevant to this process, (see Appendix 3).

Payments

Value dates

Every foreign exchange transaction has a value date. The value date is the precise date on which the host bank must deliver to its counterparty the currency which was sold to it under the contract. Similarly, the counterparty to the deal must deliver the currency (countervalue) amount purchased by the host bank on the same day (i.e. the value date). Care is needed to ensure that deals are not inadvertently written for holidays in the host country of the currency - regular updating of the database with holidays is necessary to avoid unnecessary reprocessing. Most automated systems will usually highlight any deals dealt for an apparent holiday for one or other of the currencies involved and require 'a manual override' if it is to be ignored. EMU has reduced settlements holidays in EUR to a minimum, but holidays are not yet set immutably for every year.

It is imperative that the host bank executes payment of the sold currency on the exact date agreed in the contract. Failure to do so will result in an interest claim being lodged on the host bank by the counterparty for late receipt of its funds. Similarly, where the host bank is due to receive funds from its counterparty into a nostro (or vostro) account, it is also imperative that the funds are received on the contracted value date. Upon reconciling nostro (and vostro) accounts, failure to notice that incoming funds have been received late or outgoing payments have been effected with an earlier value date than instructed, will result in overdraft interest charges being incurred. The introduction of the euro has put some extra pressure on the back office since value same day and value tomorrow transactions will increase significantly.

Maturity dates

Whereas a spot foreign exchange deal has only one value date, being the date on which the two currencies must be exchanged by the buyer and seller, there are exceptions.

Spot is usually 2 working days after the deal date - with the exception of CAD which works on a trade +1 settlement date. The one currency where care is needed re 2 separate settlement dates for a spot trade is SAR. Given the religious holidays in the Middle East, SAR cannot be settled on a Friday. Trades, however, do take place on a Wednesday, thus SAR might be settled Saturday and USD Friday, or both on the following Monday, or USD Friday and SAR Saturday. For the 1st and 3rd of these alternatives the rate will have to be adjusted to allow for the non-simultaneous settlement of the funds.

In the case of an FX swap, there is both the spot and the forward date for both currencies to be settled.

In a money market deal there are also two value dates. The first value date is the date on which the lender of the monies must deliver the currency to the borrower. The second value date is the date on which the borrower of the monies must return the principal amount, together with all accrued interest, to the lender. This second value date in money market parlance is known officially as the *maturity date*.

Payment methods

One of the most important aspects of the deal process is the outgoing payment. The way the payment is made will depend on how well integrated the host bank's systems are, as well as how automated its payment system is. With the use of the latest technology and by using SSIs, highly automated banks can achieve straight-through processed rates in the region of 80% - 90%. In other words, once the deal is struck and it passes a series of automated validity checks, a confirmation and payment order can be automatically generated and merely awaits final (human) verification before being released.

Normally, such confirmations (MT300/MT320) and payments (MT100/MT202/MT203) are sent via the SWIFT network. SWIFT, or the Society for World-wide Interbank Financial Telecommunications, was established in 1977. It is owned by a consortium of international banks and owes much of its success to the standardisation of financial messages such as confirmations, payments, statements and advices. SWIFT operates in 5,300 financial institutions in over 137 countries and continues to grow.

Each field or piece of data on a SWIFT message has an internationally recognised reference number and each field must be structured in a particular manner thereby helping to make all SWIFT messages easily understood. It is vital that the correct message form is used per transaction type as the cancelling of a SWIFT message and/or the return of funds will always have its problems - especially where 'use of funds' compensation is requested by the institution which incorrectly paid funds. (In the USA standard rules now apply to any such request regarding 'undue enrichment', covering reserve requirements and penalty charges per transaction.)

Banks which do not use SWIFT Accord or subscribe to one of many alternative systems - e.g. ACS, Comfort - must continue to use the postal service for sending confirmations and to use tested telexes for executing their payment orders. A tested telex is one which is authenticated by the sender to ensure the security and authenticity of the message (see later section, Cash Management, on page 65). Telexes, however, are rarely used in major financial centresnowadays.

Deadlines

For the majority of the world's currencies which are traded in the foreign exchange and money markets, it is normally sufficient to give one day's notice of payment from the sending/ordering bank to the receiving/paying bank. In other words if, for example, a CHF payment order was being sent by a UK bank to a bank in Switzerland for value Monday 21/10, the payment order should be sent from the British bank to the Swiss bank by the close of business on the 18/10 to ensure that the beneficiary receives good value 21/10.

Most deadlines for the payment of currencies for value the same day are before 12 midday on the value date (USD and GBP are notable exceptions), but it is imperative that back office staff are aware of all deadlines by currency. A payment deadline or cut-off time is the latest time which the payment order can be received by the paying bank from the ordering bank to guarantee that good value will be applied to the beneficiary's account.

Note that particular agents (Clearstream/Euroclear/CHIPS or CHAPS) have their own requirement. For example, the rules for CHAPS state that a payment received by a bank, which it is unable to apply, must be returned by it to the remitter by 12 noon on the following business day in order to avoid incurring cost. It is essential the back office staff are aware of such matters, especially when changes of staff/holidays occur.

The deadline becomes very important over Easter and especially at Christmas and New Year when different countries have different holidays, and cut-off times are often varied to allow for these and the fact that banks work on skeleton staff. For settlements in the euro, TARGET initially only closed on Christmas day and New Year's day - since 1999 they have varied each year. For up-to-date information always check www.ebs.com.

Receipt of payment orders after the deadline will (usually) result in the payment being executed on the next available business day. In such cases, the ordering bank will receive an interest claim from the beneficiary bank for the late receipt of funds and this will result in a monetary loss to the ordering bank.

The back office must therefore always be aware of the respective cut-off times for the various traded currencies. Also, some individual banks may impose their deadlines which may differ from the generally accepted deadlines in that country.

Netting

Although the overall concept of netting is valid - i.e. avoiding gross settlement of each individual trade and thereby reducing the volume of trades to be settled and the concomitant settlement risk - it adds a further onus on the back office. Netting is also a tool for reducing risk.

The choice of netting can vary considerably:

- **bilateral**: two banks, one centre, one currency; two banks, one centre, more than one currency; two banks, one currency, more than one centre and two banks, all centres more than one currency - which result in one payment, per counterparty, per currency per day (e.g. FXNet)

- **multilateral**: which implies that there are more than 2 counterparties offsetting their mutual payments/receipts via a central clearing system/clearing house where all members can net both gross or already bilaterally netted positions. Such a system would result in just one payment, per currency, per day from each member. ECHO in Europe was operational and Multinet in North America was about to become operational when CLS Ltd bought them out with a view to inaugurating a global multilateral system.

After a delay of 3 years from due date and a vastly increased budget, CLS opened for business on 11th September 2002. However, it is still not complete and true to its originally planned format - number of currencies or centres plugged in. Don't hold your breath.

CLS is supported by 67 banks and an investment of $300 + million. There are 39 clearing members (expected to be 50 by end of 2003) covering 80% of the world's FX business by value. An estimated 97% reduction in numbers of payment instructions will be made.

Initial data on put-through is encouraging - USD 5 trillion was processed in the first 8 weeks, with a 100% settlement rate covering 30,000 payment instructions - so more banks may join. New members are subject to a rigorous testing and trialing programme to ensure their systems and processes are compatible with CLS and meet the operational requirements of CLS Bank.

Key features of CLS are:

* Bilateral settlement daily gross reduced to 5-hour multilateral settlement on a payment versus payment basis on books of CLS Bank. It holds a multicurrency account for each member and a RTGS account with each of 7 Central Banks.

* 70 CLS shareholders, 7 currencies - USD;GBP;CAD;EUR;JPY;CHF and AUD.

* Benefits in reduced liquidity costs, STP and reduction in reconciliation problems

* Swedish Krona, Danish Kroner and Norwegian Krone plus Singapore Dollars are due to join in 2003 and possibly New Zealand Dollars.

* CLS Bank is based in New York and regulated by the Federal Reserve Bank of New York

In essence, only an automated netting system can work without placing undue stress on the human factor. Payment netting involving two counterparties results in the offsetting of funds payable to and receivable from each other to arrive at a situation where only one net payment is made (per currency).

Types of netting

In addition to the settlement basis of netting described above, banks entering into such netting arrangements have other choices:

1. simple payment netting

2. netting by novation

1. Simple payment netting lacks a fundamental insurance - that of a client going bust and its 'clever' lawyers picking out only the deals profitable to its client to settle whilst ignoring those which would incur a loss for its client - the so-called 'cherry-picking' exercise.

2. Netting by novation avoids the possible problems of (1) by establishing that all deals being netted are cancelled and replaced by a new (nova) legally binding deal

n.b. If using ISDA documentation to include netting, back office must specifically adopt 'netting by novation', as currently it is only simple payment netting that is included.

Close-out netting

Back office should only become involved in close-out netting once a decision has been made elsewhere. For close-out netting only comes into force when a counterparty goes bankrupt and/or defaults or chooses to have all deals cancelled and revalued whilst still solvent. Outstanding contracts and mark-to-market prices for those positions are then obtained (see page 115 for a detailed example).

Clearing and payment systems

Clearing

In the majority of cases, when a bank is settling a foreign currency transaction, it will use the services provided by its nostro account bank to execute the payment in favour of the beneficiary. However, where the payment is to be made to the beneficiary in local currency, normally, the local payment clearing system is used. Individual clearing systems may be owned and operated by a consortium of local banks or they may be operated and controlled by a country's central bank.

In essence, the function of the clearing house from where the clearing system operates is to allow each member bank to settle daily all monies payable to and receivable from all other members of that payment clearing system. Rather than physically make hundreds of payments to each other every day, the net position (funds receivable against funds payable) is calculated for each bank with each other member and each bank would then either receive or make only one payment to every other member of the clearing.

In the USA, the USD clearing system is known as CHIPS or Clearing House Interbank Payment System. In the UK, the clearing system is known as CHAPS or Clearing House Automated Payments System. Each country has its own local payment clearing system which is usually located in the main financial centre or the capital city. All clearing systems have their own rules and regulations devised to ensure fair and efficient running. For example, the rules for CHAPS state that a payment received by a bank, which it is unable to apply, must be returned by it to the remitter by 12 noon on the following business day in order to avoid incurring cost. CHAPS is one of three clearing companies that forms the Association for Payment Clearing Services (APACS). CHAPS only accounts for 0.3% of APACS' volumes but 92% of value. BACS (Banks

Automated Clearing Services) and Cheque & Credit Clearing Company are the other two.

Banks which are not members of their local payments clearing system must employ the services of a bank which is a member in order to execute their own payments in the local currency.

Settlements in Euro

Since the creation of the euro banks have had the choice of either belonging to TARGET or to EBA (the major clearers) - plus the 4 other significant services:

German system	EAF
UK Euro	CHAPS
French	PNS
Spanish	SEPI

Membership of **TARGET** is open to any bank in the 12 'in' countries. It has over 5,000 members, but their **accounts have to always be in credit**.

EBA's system - EURO1 - allows membership to any EU Member State and concentrates on cross-border payments. Multilateral maximum debit and credit limits apply between members.

Intraday overdrafts are allowed within this closed system where, at the end of the trading day, 'short' banks settle by a single payment into TARGET, where - on instructions from the EBA - they distribute payment to the 'long' banks. The sum of all short positions is equal to the sum of all long positions.

Bridges exist between TARGET and EBA for security held in one system to be used in the other. Similarly arrangements exist between members of either EAF or PNS to provide liquidity to their local RTGS systems.

n.b. EAF and PNS are not Real Time Gross Settlement systems (RTGS)

> TARGET is the international settlement system between each country for euros whilst EBA runs the settlement between each bank in euros before net settlement is entered into TARGET.

All times CET	TARGET & CHAPS euro	EBA	EAF
Opening	07.00	07.30	07.00
Customer cut-off (a) Inputs (b) Debits	17.00 By 17.07:30		
Interbank cut-off: (a) Inputs (b) Debits	18.00 By 18.07:30	16.00	16.00
Reconciliation/ settlement complete	Around 18.30	Around 16.45	16.30

Note: (a) by SWIFT MT100 or equivalent national message format: (b) by SWIFT MT202 or equivalent national message format

The **EURO1 system** provides an efficient, secure and cost-effective method to facilitate end-to-end processing of payment messages denominated in euro.

The system rests on:

- A continuous balance calculation and limit check;
- A highly automated settlement arrangement with the European Central Bank;
- A service which monitors the payments traffic in the system, intervening where circumstances may affect the smooth performance of the system, and manages the settlement process;
- A clearing workstation for front-end information.

Calculation of debit and credit cap

Each participant extends to each other participant a mandatory limit of EUR 5 million.

- In addition to the EUR 5 million limit, each participant may grant at its discretion a limit of up to EUR 25 million, totalling a maximum of EUR 30 million bilateral risk per participant.

- The debit cap of a participant is the sum of the limits received from the other participants. The credit cap of a participant is the sum of the limits given to the other participants.

- For reasons of limiting systemic risk, a participant's debit and credit cap may not exceed EUR 1 billion.

Summary - EBA/TARGET

• Banks can be members of either or both. Criteria for membership have to be satisfied.

• TARGET is not restricted to banks from within the Euro area.

• TARGET accounts must always be in credit.

• TARGET is real-time - your account is debited and the Central Bank in the country of the payee is credited. You will receive notification that the ultimate beneficiary has been credited.

• TARGET cut-off is 4pm for MT100 and 5pm for MT 202, London time.

• EBA - only has 60-70 banks (TARGET has thousands) but can have daylight agreed overdraft. Collateral is required so in a default situation you could have to contribute in something.

• EBA payments are direct from the paying to the receiving bank.

Vostro accounts

Treasury business is undertaken in the majority of the world's major currencies and the use of nostro accounts for the settlement of cross-border payments is described in Chapter 4. In the same way that a host bank needs to own and operate a nostro account held overseas to settle its foreign currency transactions, banks overseas have an identical need to effect cross-border payments in the host bank's local currency. Therefore, if, for example, a bank in the USA opened an account with a bank located in the UK and that account was denominated in pounds sterling, that account in the UK is known as a vostro account. Therefore, a vostro account is essentially the name given by the host bank to an account owned by an overseas bank and maintained in the host bank's local currency. The bank overseas in turn refers to this as their Nostro

e.g. Standard Chartered Bank London opens a CHF account at UBS, Zurich. This account would be referred to by Standard Chartered as their CHF Nostro. UBS, Zurich in their books would call it a Vostro account in CHF held for Standard Chartered, London.

A bank may own more than one nostro account, usually for operational purposes - one for FX settlements, one for MM. Responsibility for ensuring adequate funding on foreign currency accounts lies with the holder/owner of that account as overdraft interest charges can be incurred on them.

Joining the CLS Bank system allows participating banks to cut down the number of nostros required and thus the funds tied up in liquidity costs to fund them.

Herstatt risk

The need of each bank to execute its foreign currency payment orders in advance of known cut-off times, normally involves the despatching of its payment orders to its nostro correspondent bank at least one day prior to the required value date.

Herstatt risk refers to each situation where a bank in one country effecting a payment in favour of a bank in another country is faced with the possibility that, overnight, the counterparty to the transaction to whom the funds were paid, is unable to settle its side of the (e.g. foreign exchange) transaction owing to bankruptcy being declared by that counterparty.

Herstatt Bank was a medium-sized West German bank which, in 1974, became insolvent and was therefore unable to meet its payment commitments to its international counterparty banks who had already paid funds to it without the knowledge of Herstatt Bank's impending bankruptcy.

All banks run this risk and attempt to reduce the potential for loss in this way. By setting maximum dealing limits with each of their counterparties with whom they trade, a bank can reduce its exposure to individual banks. Many banks also join payment netting schemes which mitigate the potential for loss owing to Herstatt risk, as the sums due from and payable to each counterparty are netted out, thereby reducing their actual exposure to that bank. Additionally, by delaying the transmission of their payment order from a spot (or earlier) date to just one day prior to the value date, this further reduces the possibility of monetary loss owing to Herstatt risk.

Essentially, therefore, Herstatt Risk is synonymous with delivery/settlement risk.

Non-standard settlement instruments

Certificates of deposit (CDs)

Primary CDs - i.e. when first issued as an acknowledgement of a deposit received - are treated as an Interbank Fixed Deposit. When, however, they are bought/sold during their life a regular, but slightly more complicated, function of the back office is required. Other negotiable instruments (commercial paper, banker's acceptances and Treasury bills) also come into this area. However, once the formula is mastered, there is merely a mechanical calculation to be done.

Depending on the currency, there may be a secondary function required - that of arranging delivery. To avoid the need to have the physical transfer of bearer instruments arranged - some robberies have occurred in the past - in London for USD securities, First Chicago Clearing Centre (FCCC) operates a depository, and for GBP securities, the Bank of England operates the Central Moneymarkets Office (CMO)* for bills and CDs and the Central Gilts Office (CGO)* for gilts and £ debentures. The settlement procedure is 90% DVP (delivery versus payment) - i.e. delivery or advice to the depository to move the security to the new owner will release the actual cash.

---

* both the CMO and CGO are now operated by CrestCo on behalf of the Bank of England

Calculation of proceeds of secondary market CD

To use formula for Secondary Market Proceeds:

First calculate maturity proceeds:

$$\text{Maturity proceeds} = \text{face value} \times \left\{ 1 + \left[\text{coupon rate} \times \frac{\text{days from issue to maturity}}{\text{daybase}} \right] \right\}$$

Now substitute in new formula:

$$\text{Secondary market proceeds} = \frac{\text{maturity proceeds}}{\left\{ 1 + \left[\text{yield} \times \frac{\text{days left to mature}}{\text{daybase}} \right] \right\}}$$

Thus, if the maturity value of a CD is CAD 5,203,333.33, a methodology has to be devised to identify a sale price for the instruments which will satisfy the buyer's need for an investment yielding 7.5%.

$$\frac{mp}{\left\{ 1 + \left[y \times \frac{d_{tm}}{db} \right] \right\}} = \frac{5.203,333.33}{\left\{ 1 + \left[.075 \times \frac{91}{360} \right] \right\}} = \frac{5,203,333.33}{1.0189583} = 5,106,522.30$$

Discounted instruments

These are commercial paper, Treasury bills and banker's acceptances, where the face value (FV) is discounted so that the amount paid away by the lender is always less than face value. The back office's role, under today's degree of mechanisation, would be limited to random checks that the correct formula has been applied. Thus, for UK bills - mostly issued for three or six months in face values of GBP 1,000,000 - if we take a 90-day issue at 10%, using the appropriate formula the proceeds will be:

$$\text{Proceeds} = FV - \left[FV \left(\frac{T \times DR}{B \times 100} \right) \right]$$

$$= 1,000,000 - \left[1,000,000 \left(\frac{90 \times 10}{36500} \right) \right]$$

$$= 1,000,000 - 24,657.53 = 975,342.47$$

where:	FV	=	Face Value
	T	=	Time
	DR	=	Discount Rate
	B	=	Base (360 or 365 days)

Non-deliverable forwards

In pure foreign exchange terms, non-deliverable forwards (NDFs) have allowed speculation in a currency's future value which could not otherwise be achieved since there were restrictions on what transactions qualified for forward cover (i.e. trade only) or the market was illiquid. The currencies tend to be the more exotic currencies, for example, Mexican peso, Malaysian ringgit, Indonesian rupiah, etc.

After a forward price has been agreed between the two counterparties, either the market user can go back before maturity and settle just the difference between the original contract rate and the rate now current for that date, (this leaves you open to being 'read') or you wait until the original forward date and then offset at difference spot/original contract rate.

Example - buyer of NDF in $ amount

If the fixing rate is greater than the outright price at maturity, the purchaser of the NDF will receive from the seller the difference between the fixing rate and the outright rate in cash terms. This amount can be calculated as follows:

$$\frac{(F - O) \times N}{F}$$

where F = fixing rate, O = outright price and N = notional amount. Obviously, if the fixing rate is less than the outright price at maturity, the opposite will apply.

Sale example

Notional amount	USD 10,000,000.00
Maturity	90 days
Spot	2.0000 FX/USD
90-day NDF	0.0100
Outright	2.0100 FX/USD
Fixing rate	2.0200 FX/USD

At maturity the purchase of the NDF will receive from the seller:

$$(2.0200 - 2.0100 \times USD\ 10,000,000.00)$$

$$2.0200$$

$$0.0100 \times 10,000,000.00$$

$$2.0200$$

$$USD\ 49,504.95$$

In investment terms NDFs provide the opportunity to hedge cash flows from investments in more exotic currencies. This is becoming more important as investors look for higher returns than those available in current stable interest rate environments of Western Europe/USA/Japan and ahead of the single currency.

An investor wanting to benefit from the type of enhanced yield available in the emerging markets would have to do the following:

- Purchase the spot currency and sell dollars
- Invest in a local risk-free asset (i.e. a government bond)
- Fund the dollars at Libor
- Receive the capital plus interest at maturity
- Sell the currency on the spot market and purchase dollars

Using an NDF the investor can hedge the FX risk inherent in the investment. In doing this he can take advantage of much greater yields. For example, the implied NDF yield on the six-month New Taiwanese dollar (NTD) is 6.5% while, on the Korean won, it is 13.5%.

The back office role in this context is that of correct encoding, input and eventual settlement. An understanding of the overall concept of NDFs, however, will always assist efficiency.

Bonds

In essence, bonds are merely long-term (2-30 years) I.O.Us issued by banks, governments and international companies. Compared to simple money market settlements, the procedures required for bonds are more demanding. However, provided the bond being purchased/sold has been dealt in previously, your computer program will already have full details. If not, you will be required to enter all standing data. This is available on all bonds from either a Bloomberg/Reuters 3000Xtra screen or Euroclear. The most significant fact is that bonds are normally settled via Euroclear or Clearstream and value is three days ahead (it used to be eight days). In the future it is planned to achieve same day settlement when required - in 2002* the market had planned move to T+1 settlement. Messages therefore currently need to be sent in good time.

Day conventions can be particularly important here, but the office should have a copy of these should there be any doubt (see Appendix 12). Similarly, cross-referencing to other instruments being used as a hedge against the bond will often be required.

Most confirmations are entered into ISMA's (International Securities and Markets Association) TRAX system - the equivalent of TRAM for FX and MM. A major requirement is that every trade must be matched within half an hour of the time it was traded, otherwise there will be a fine, escalating by time. Also every bond transaction has to be reported to the supervisory body, the Securities and Futures Authority (SFA) - now part of the Financial Services Authority (FSA).

If the accounting function is part of your particular back office/support department, then accounts for the actual consideration (total price paid), dividends, redemptions and sinking fund will be required.

Derivative settlements

The use - or rather misuse - of derivatives has led to comments like the following: 'A derivative is like a razor. You can use it shave yourself and make yourself attractive for your girlfriend. You can slit her throat with it. Or you can use it to commit suicide.' 'Derivatives have been likened to aspirin; taken for a headache, they will make the pain go away. If you take the whole bottle at once you may kill yourself.' (Financial Times, 4 March 1995.)

It has also led to losses such as these:

- Metallgesellchaft - US$1.5/2 billion
- Procter & Gamble - £69 million
- Atlantic Richfield - US$22 million
- Barings Bank - £820 million
- Orange County in California - US$3 to 5 billion
- Hammersmith and Fulham - £80 million
- LTCM - US$8 billion

Whilst these are examples of front office and/or management misuse, back office equally has to be most vigilant in its role/responsibility for monitoring and settling such transactions.

---

* Now postponed

The past 10 to 15 years have seen an explosive growth in the volumes of derivative products traded under the relatively new science known as financial engineering. There is a wide variety of such products available for both speculative and hedging purposes. In essence, a derivative product is a financial instrument which was *derived* from another core financial product based on an interest or an exchange rate (see Table 3.1).

Derivatives were developed to help financial institutions and investment professionals to better manage their investment strategies. These instruments have names such as caps, collars, floors, options, swaps, interest rate swaps, swaptions and currency options, to name but a few. Some, such as futures, are highly standardised in terms of amounts and maturities whilst others, such as options, can be tailor-made to suit individual clients. Additionally, some can only be traded in highly regulated markets known as exchanges, while others can be traded in the Over The Counter (OTC) market.

Derivatives can be used either by companies which are risk-averse, in order to lock into an exchange or interest thereby reducing their exposure to interest and/or exchange rate fluctuations, or they can be used by investors to speculate on commodities and even on the stock market.

FRAs

Future rate agreements (FRAs) were one of the first derivatives to be developed, and were the replacement for forward/forward interest rates. The latter were very difficult to arrange and only a few banks would quote them despite the need for treasurers to be able to hedge interest rate risk they knew they would have in the future. Together with the effect on the balance sheet and the filling-up of limits, the need led to the introduction of FRAs. As far as back office is concerned, involvement is required at both the arrangement of the FRA - confirming dates, rate, amount, etc., - and at maturity (the actual start date of the FRA) when the settlement amount has to be agreed (on FRABBA terms) and paid.

Let's look at an example, using the formula in Appendix 11.

Example

If a USD 20,000,000 FRA was sold at 7.10 for a 6/12 period and LIBOR is eventually fixed at 6.57, what amount of interest is payable/receivable?

$$\frac{(7.10 - 6.57) \times 183 \times 20{,}000{,}000}{(183 \times 7.10) + (360 \times 100)} = \frac{1{,}939{,}800{,}000}{37{,}299.30} = 52{,}006.33792$$

Table 3.1 - The historical impetus to the growth of derivatives

	Developments	Innovations
1982	Reagan recovery	Philadelphia Exchange, currency options, currency swaps
1981	Federal Reserve to target money and not interest rates	LIFFE, Big Bang hits London
1980		
1979		NY Futures Exchange
1978	European Monetary System	
1977	Another attempt at exchange rate stability: Jamaica accords	NY Mercantile Exchange energy futures
1976	Recession	
1975	Volatile interest rates	Interest rate futures
1974	Commodity price swings	Growing interest in commodity futures
1973	Managed floating rates	
1972	End of gold convertibility	
1971	Collapse of Bretton Woods	Chicago Mercantile Exchange currency futures

Currency options

Back office participation only occurs in as much as agreeing the terms of such options and ensuring the premium is paid/received and the resultant processing is done. For, at maturity, either the option expires worthless - nothing to be done by back office - or the option is exercised. Exercise means that a spot transaction will be written between the bank and the holder which will be settled in the normal way for that type of transaction.

What, in the context of the mutual co-operation between front and back office, is important is that certain attributes of options contracts are understood - i.e. if a customer tries to exercise a European option other than at maturity, it is not allowed. In contrast, an American style option can be exercised at any time during the life of that deal.

Futures

These exist both as currency and interest rate futures, but it is really only the interest rate futures that have had any impact in Europe. The reason is that currency futures do not offer a significant advantage, in terms of the use of capital, over forward foreign exchange. Interest rate futures do offer much more versatility against straight cash - no principal is exchanged, good leverage is acquired via cost of initial margin compared to the size of contract owned - and thus are more popular. (see Fig 3.1 for an example of growth.)

Because financial futures can only be traded on regulated exchanges and the relevant exchange is counterparty to every contract, there is no counterparty risk of default. However, because of this, the underlying instrument is 'marked-to-market' (or revalued) on a daily basis which may necessitate the counterparty making a variation margin payment to the exchange to reflect the notionally reduced value of the underlying asset being traded - this is where the back office support is required. (There is a list of some of the contracts on LIFFE in Appendix 14.)

The back office has several duties in connection with these interest rate futures:

- Keeping a track of dealer's positions.
- Reconciling dealer's positions to statements received from agents (independent revaluation from Reuters pages for 'settlement' price).
- Managing the margin account.

Fig 3.1 - LIFFE futures and options average daily volume

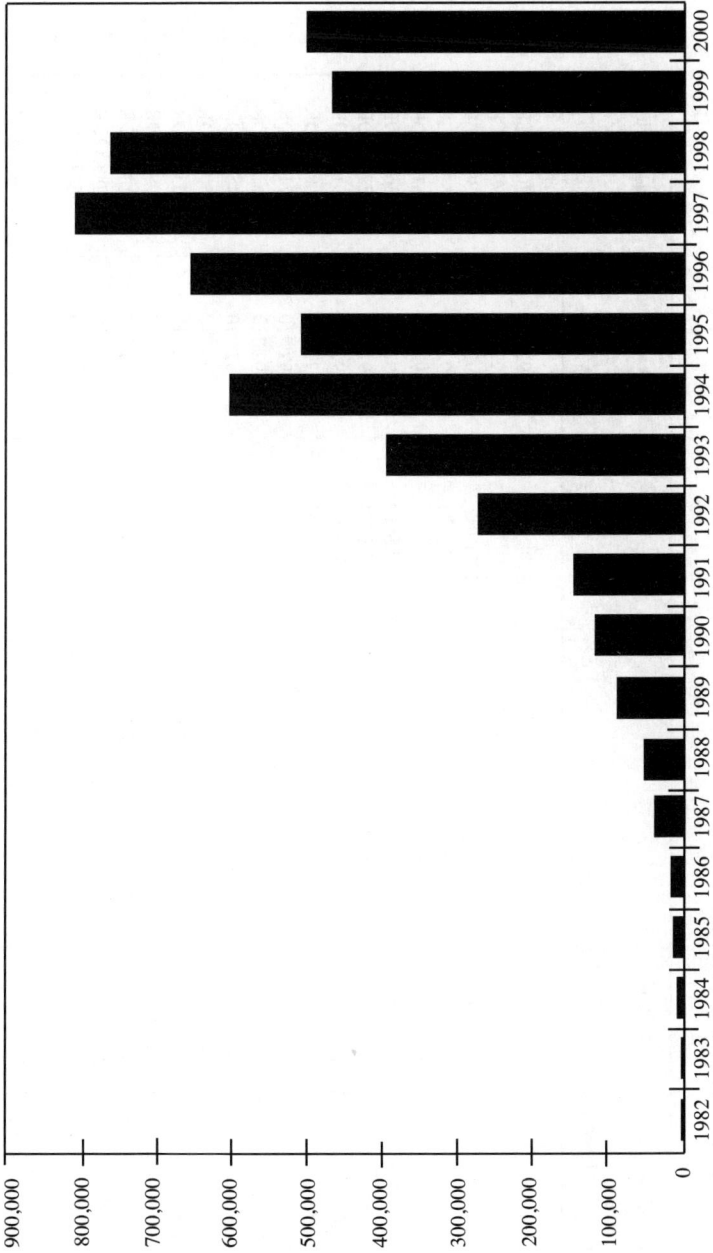

Let's look at an example - Table 3.2.

Table 3.2 - A margining example

Del month 10-year treasury bond	Trade date	Price	Lots	Reference	Market price	Margin value
Mar99	20.12.96	92.430 B	2	INTF105	92.710	4702.84CR
Mar99	06.01.97	92.230 B	65	@INT SSP1	92.710	259793.95CR
Mar99	08.01.97	92.335 B	14	INTF102	92.710	43910.86R
Mar99	17.01.97	92.540 B	15	INT F101	92.710	21515.55CR
Mar99	17.02.07	92.725 B	4	*	92.710	510.28DR
Mar99	13.01.97	92.440 S	20	INT SSP1	92.710	45368.20DR
Mar99	15.01.97	92.395 S	9	INT F101	92.710	23772.51DR
Mar99	15.01.97	92.405 S	7	INT F101	92.710	17910.41DR
Mar99	21.01.97	92.580 S	11	INT F105	92.710	12086.25DR
Mar99	30.01.97	92.425 S	12	*	92.710	28714.80DR
Mar99	03.02.97	92.520 S	16	*	92.710	25628.00DR
Mar99	03.02.97	92.585 S	8	*	92.710	8453.76DR
Mar99	04.02.97	92.625 S	30	*	92.710	21594.00DR
Mar99	04.02.97	92.635 S	1	*	92.710	635.35DR
Mar99	05.02.97	92.615 S	8	*	92.710	5083.12DR
Mar99	06.02.97	92.635 S	25	*	92.710	20103.50DR
Mar99	07.02.97	92.625 S	8	*	92.710	5083.12DR
Mar99	10.02.97	92.625 S	37	*	92.710	26632.60DR
Mar99 Futures	Total	100B	192S			88347.26CR
Futures	Total	100B	192S			88347.26CR
Total						88347.26CR

The points that are relevant to the back office are the checking that: outstandings agree to dealer's records, any reference is correctly stated and any additional margin is paid if the account falls below the minimum.

Late 1998 provided another warning on the dangers of a lack of management control on derivatives. It might have led to something approaching local systemic failure since the situation could have brought down a number of other participants in LIFFE.

The case in question concerned Griffin Trading Company, an American-owned company, where, as a result of the unauthorised trading of one dealer, losses of £6.2 million were incurred. The position taken by the trader - 9,000 DEM government bond futures - exceeded his trading limit by a factor of 10. According to the investigations of LIFFE, the SFA and the German and American authorities, something went wrong internally at the company itself and at the company processing its orders, both of whom should have realised that the positions were well outside of the authority to trade.

Since this company dealt on behalf of others, two trading companies and up to 100 individuals could have lost substantial amounts as a result of this incident. Assuming the deal(s) had been written up, back office must bear some responsibility for not bringing the matter to the attention of management (echoes of Barings and Nick Leeson's trading).

Interest rate swaps

These were 'invented' to help treasurers manage their long-term borrowings (liability swaps) and investments (asset swaps) by allowing them to make a judgement against the future direction and relationship of short to long interest rates. Thus, if they only had access to short-dated six month funds, but felt it would be better to borrow long dated funds which they thought were about to rise, then they would 'pay' in (say) the five year fixed and swap it for their six month funds. The opposite could also occur (see Fig 3.2, for example).

Back office involvement again would only be to agree rates between counterparties - and any intermediaries - and to communicate and agree with the counterparty the rollover rate each six months against the London inter bank offered rate (Libor) and exchange any difference (interest only). A variation which involves more care is a currency interest rate swap (CIRS) where the currencies for the fixed and floating currencies are not the same. In this case, an exchange of currencies may

Fig 3.2 - A basic asset swap

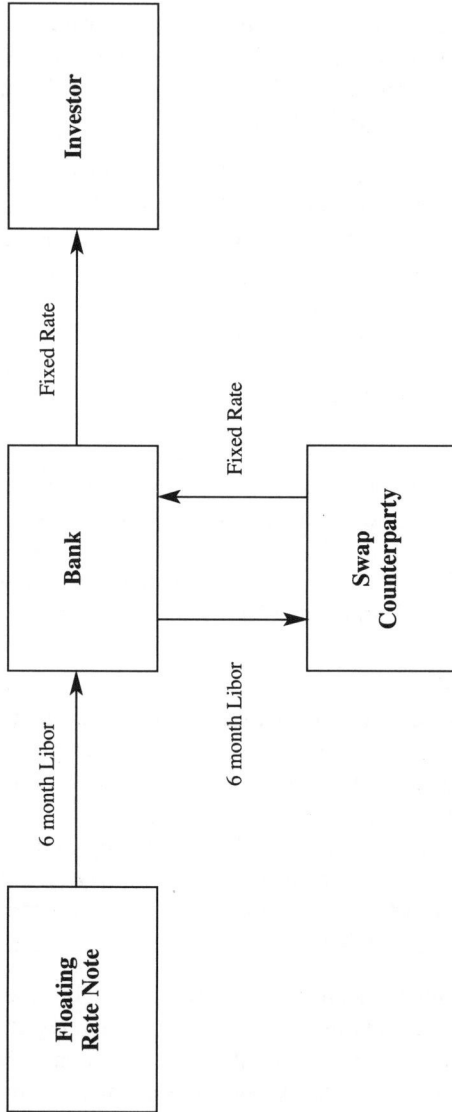

occur at the start date of the swap or at start and maturity - *there will always be an exchange at maturity.* Back office staff need to be vigilant as one CIRS may differ from another. Also, the exchange rate must be the same at the start and at maturity.

What will be vital is that any documentation called for in conjunction with the swap is received. Normally this will be ISDA since that is now the benchmark. However, some will be individually drawn up and some could be BBAIRS.

Here, the asset starts as a floating rate note, but is sold on by the bank as a 'synthetic' fixed rate bond. This is achieved by the intermediary Bank entering into a swap with a third party (swap counterparty) to change the floating rate flow into fixed, thus allowing the fixed rate to be passed on, whilst using the floating rate proceeds from the FRN to satisfy the requirement to pay floating rate to the swap counterparty.

If an institution is involved in a lot of 'financial engineering' where a bond, an IRS and some futures deals are all linked, then it will fall to the back office to ensure that the correct cross-referencing is effected - or at least that some entries have been made by front office indicating whether there are any links so that correct positions show in the position reports, management reports and P&L reports.

Caps/Floors/Collars/Corridors

Caps

A cap is essentially a series of borrowers' options, guaranteeing the maximum rate a borrower would have to pay over the whole life of a loan agreement. The basis on which they are agreed can be on LIBOR rates, commercial bill rates, prime rate and T-Bills - LIBOR is the most common. The terms can extend over 10 years over a wide choice of currencies, reset levels (1/3/6 monthly) at any strike (usually quoted in half-percents with the premium expressed as a percentage of the notional amount paid up front).

Floors

This would be the converse of a cap, thereby being the equivalent of a series of put options guaranteeing a minimum interest rate yield.

Collars

A collar involves the simultaneous purchase of a cap with a sale of a floor. In this way the buyer is trying to reduce overall cost by giving up some of the potential benefit of a favourable move in rates. Thus the buyer of the collar is both guaranteeing himself a maximum cost of borrowing whilst offsetting the premium cost by selling a floor. This could be made into a zero-cost option if the levels of the two strikes suited the buyer. - e.g. collar buyer could buy collar for two year period at 8% and sell floor at 7.5% - both at 3 month rollovers - at zero cost if premium paid on one and earned on other was the same (say .75%). The buyer thereby fixes the cost as minimum of 7.5% and maximum of 8% but has given up the benefit of rates below 7.5%.

The biggest difference between a collar and a cap or floor is that both parties assume credit risk on each other. Collars can be compared to an IRS and sometimes may be cheaper, especially if short:long rates have a very large differential. Thus if a collar is set at a 10% cap and a 6% floor, interest would not change hands unless rates for the period concerned were less than 6% or more than 10%.

Corridor

Very similar to a collar but involves the simultaneous purchases of a cap at one strike with a sale at a higher level. This is merely another way of reducing premium by giving up some of the advantage of a major upwards move in rates.

Payment

Unlike short term derivatives, any difference payable on a cap or floor is payable in arrears at the end of the period on which the difference is due, using a simple interest formula. The premium is calculated as a flat amount. Thus $5,000,000 protected at 9% would require a premium of $45,000 payable up front.

Repurchase agreements (repos)

Outside the USA, repurchase agreements were slow to take off, but they now exist wherever there is a developed bond market. Their use to a bond holder is to earn interest on the investment, while to a borrower it is to obtain cheap short-date funding. The mechanics are that repos are arranged for very short periods where the owner (holder) 'lends' the bond for which the temporary borrower pays an interest rate which is used to calculate the difference between the price on the bond when sold and the rate on it when it is returned to the original owner.

The difficulty for back office emanates from the different types of repo operation - sell/buy-back; classic repo or securities lending - and the various ancillary duties - arrangements for delivery, margin calls and payment peculiarities. This will necessitate at least a basic understanding of the different types and their 'jargon'. Examples of each type, with variations are included in Appendix 6. However, the essential points to be grasped by back office are as follows:

- The movement of the bond being used as collateral/calculation of delivery proceeds.
- Haircuts.
- The treatment of coupons.
- The 'margin' receipt/payment during the life of repo.
- The settlement will normally be via Clearstream or Euroclear (see Appendix 4).
- The selection of appropriate documentation.

Whatever the style of the repo agreement, remember:

a) The bond used in the repo is also known as the security or the collateral.

b) The repoer is also known as the seller of the security / bond / collateral, or the taker of the cash.

c) The reverse repoer is also known as the buyer of the security / bond / collateral, or the giver of the cash.

Delivery

Traditionally, this issue has been taken rather lightly by the market. No doubt, the cost and aggravation involved in what was initially an overnight market had a lot to do with it. The practice of 'holding to order' or 'held in custody' became commonplace and was generally accepted in the market. However, as the repo became a more popular instrument so the opportunities for fraud became easier.

A series of high profile frauds in the United States culminating with the Wallace Smith Trust scandal in Canada in 1991 emphasised the problem, and led to a general market practice of delivery versus payment (DVP).

This means exactly what it reads and is further facilitated by the services of the various clearing agencies, both international and domestic. i.e. whoever you use to hold security will work out whether what you want to deliver is in your portfolio and its delivery price. Bloomberg and Reuters 3000Xtra screens also do this.

Essentially, whereas the dealer is only interested in the trading (clean) price, the back office has to deliver on the basis of the dirty price (clean price adjusted by accrued interest since last coupon payment)

Tri-party repo

Tri-party is a transaction in which both counterparts use the same custodian, and in which segregated accounts are opened specifically for the purpose of repo transactions between the two institutions. All the administration is carried out by the custodian under parameters included within a legally binding agreement signed by all three parties.

Haircuts

Margins, known colloquially as haircuts, are required primarily to protect the provider of the cash from any deterioration in the value of the collateral during the period of the repo. Thus if an investment bank wanted to raise cash to the total USD 100 million and a 2% margin was required they would have to make collateral worth USD 102 million available. Obviously if the price of the securities was below par they would have to provide even more collateral so that the real value was always above USD 102 million.

For the margin system to be efficient, one has to be certain that the collateral has been set aside correctly in the first place, and also that its real value is monitored and adjusted during the life of the repo transaction. The arrival of the tri-party agreement has made the management of the margin a much more straightforward task and has a lot to do with the increase in the size of the market in recent years.

Obviously, the credit standing of the paper used as collateral affects the size of the margin. Collateral with an AA rating might enjoy a margin of 2%, whilst collateral with a BBB rating might have a margin of at least 5%. The return will come into the equation as well, in that some investors have a bigger appetite for risk and therefore would accept a tighter margin in return for a higher rate.

Other factors that could have an impact on the size of the margin are:

- the term of the repo: in that the longer the repo has to run, the greater the chance there is of default.
- the final maturity of the collateral: a longer maturity is more susceptible to interest rate changes and, in the event of default, depending on the type of instrument, might not be so liquid.
- the credit standing of the counterpart providing the collateral.
- the liquidity of the collateral.
- whether the transaction is covered by a legal agreement.
- whether the collateral is denominated in another currency(s) to that of the cash amount.

In practice, the management of margins is not straightforward. Clearly, with a sell/buy back it is impossible to adjust the amount of the collateral without undoing the deal. Although, it has be known that counterparts will do just that especially if the term of the repo is long. This in turn, however, generally leads to higher margin requirements for sell/buy backs than it does for other types of repo.

Thus, normally one would only find the margin being adjusted on a regular basis in the case of the standard (i.e. classic) repo. This, in itself, is not straightforward in that the cost of making an adjustment for every little price movement, even on a daily basis, would make the cost prohibitive. Therefore, as part of the master agreement it will have been decided beforehand, between the two counterparts, as to how much the price can move before a margin adjustment needs to be made. This is normally included in the agreement as an amount and will reflect the type of business that is likely to be carried out. Obviously, if one is dealing in smaller amounts, e.g. USD 20.0 million, a 2% margin would mean a collateral requirement of USD 20.4 million and therefore a threshold of USD 100,000 would seem apposite. For much larger amounts the threshold could be larger itself.

How 'haircuts' work

1. If you have the collateral and wish to raise the cash, the procedure is as follows:

Nominal Value of Bond	USD 1,000,000
Dirty Price	99,00
Cash Value of Bond	USD 990,000
Haircut	2%
Amount of cash raised	USD 970,588.24

Explanation

The bond has a nominal value of USD 1 million. The dirty price indicates that if the bond is sold one would receive USD 990,000. (for every USD 100 nominal, one would receive USD 99). Because the lender of the cash wants some protection against an adverse movement in the price he asks for a margin or 'haircut', in this case 2%. Thus, for every USD 100 he requires collateral with a value of USD 102. In this instant, therefore, he is only prepared to lend USD 970,588.24 against a collateral that has a value of USD 990,000.

2. If you have the cash and wish to invest it by way of a repo, the procedure is as follows:

Cash amount	USD 1,000,000
Haircut	2%
Required Value of Bond	USD 1,020,000
Dirty Price	99.00
Nominal Value of Bond	USD 1,030,303.03

Explanation

The lender has USD 1 million.

He requires a haircut of 2% to protect himself from an adverse price movements so, whatever the security, the collateral he needs has to have a real value of USD 1,020,000.

The collateral that the seller is prepared to put up has a dirty price of 99.00. Therefore to secure an amount of USD 1,020,000. he needs to provide collateral with a nominal value of :

1,020,000 x 100/99 = USD 1,030,303.03 (for every USD 100 nominal he can raise USD 99).

Because bonds are issued in round amounts, if the minimum issue in this case was USD 1,000. the seller would have to provide bonds with a nominal value of USD 1,031,000.

Coupons

Since, to facilitate the operation of repos, legal ownership passes to the reverse repoer, it is logical that any coupon received during the life of a repo also becomes the property of the reverse repoer. What back office has to ensure is that all this takes place efficiently over their clearing accounts by issuing the correct instructions.

Margin calls

Margin calls are made by the cash lender to ensure that the value of his security never falls below the current value of cash advanced. Current value, therefore, is always principal plus interest to date when assessing this.

What can happen when a margin call is made:

1) If the repo is a sell/buy-back, there is only one possibility - settle the repo to date and begin again:

> i) same collateral, lesser amount
> ii) same amount, different collateral

2) If it is a Classic repo then:

a) lender will require additional security to match the deficit in the value originally given and value P+I to date.

b) lender will accept cash equivalent of (a) - normally at original repo rate.

c) if neither (a) or (b) is possible, then lender will require settlement to date and then choice to go on:

> iii) same collateral, lesser amount
> iv) same amount, different collateral

Documentation

The TBMA-ISMA Agreement

In general terms, the TBMA-ISMA standard agreement offers the best of both worlds to its users. On the one hand it offers a recognised framework providing adequate security to the user whilst leaving enough flexibility, through the use of its annexes, that it can be tailored to a particular situation or relationship. The document itself is the Global Master Repo Agreement (GMRA).

Once the agreement is signed by the two parties no further documentation needs to be exchanged, with the exception of the confirmation for the individual deals, the format of which having already been agreed in the master agreement.

The body of the document, although relating to the basic repo, will give the holder the right over the securities as if it were a sell/buy back transaction. This is particularly important in English law which is the jurisdiction by which the agreement is governed.

n.b. For repo transactions it is recommended that documentation is exchanged before the first transaction takes place,

Other terms relating to repo trading:

Double dipping

A fraudulent practice whereby the owner of the security uses the same collateral to raise cash from more than one counterpart for the same period.

Flex repo

A form of repo used mainly in the United States where the repayment, by agreement at the outset, is amortised over the life of the repo, the advantage being that the cash provider gets a little more flexibility with his liquidity whilst still retaining a fixed rate return.

General collateral

A term used whereby the collateral meets the general requirements of the counterpart but is not specific. It can also mean a repo that is not special.

Hold in custody

A term signifying that the security has not been delivered to the counterpart's clearer, but is held in a segregated account either at the offices of the repurchaser or its own clearer.

Open repo

A repo that has no fixed term and is automatically rolled over each day until one of the counterparts needs to close it. The rate is agreed daily. (n.b. an open repo can never be executed as a sell/buy-back, which needs a fixed start and end date).

Securities lending

A form of repo whereby a particular stock is lent to a counterpart for a specific period for which a fee is charged. The collateral is usually in the form of other securities but can also be cash. It usually arises as the result of a failure in the delivery of securities in the wider market. Also known as stock lending in the UK.

Specials

a) A bond 'goes' special when a number of market participants are short of a specific security. This can make borrowing money against the stock particularly cheap for a holder - i.e. the holders can borrow money at rates well below the market level.

b) Securities that are deliverable against the maturity of a bond futures contract.

Substitution

The replacement of collateral during the term of the repo at the discretion of the counterpart that has provided the cash. Under a tri-party repo this process is allowed for in the documentation and is therefore more straightforward.

System repo

A repo by which the Federal Reserve Bank of New York adds liquidity to the market thus influencing short term interest rates.

CHAPTER 4

▌▌▌

POST-SETTLEMENT
DUTIES

Confirmations

The duty of confirmations is, of course, not solely post-settlement, as automation has intervened via Accord/Comfort/TRAX etc., as have standard settlement instructions (SSIs). SWIFT users normally exchange confirmations using MT300 or MT320 messages. Highly automated banks can use these standardised messages to facilitate automatic matching of incoming confirmations. Similarly, many FX/MM brokers in Europe can also send their confirmations electronically into one of the many automated matching systems, and this also facilitates automatic matching by the recipients of their confirmations (see Appendix 3 for full details).

The system effectively short-cuts the delivery of paper-based confirmations, which would need separate generation and physical delivery to the counterparty, by providing automatic electronic messages from the broker to the bank as the details are entered at the broker's office. The speed of transmission is especially useful for short-date transactions where payments have to be made almost immediately after the deal has been completed - although see Chapter 3 concerning London banks' practice on short dates. All of these can be used together with your own in-house computer or paper-based systems and the advantages are as follows:

- Speed of reconciliation.
- Reduction in boring procedures (which often result in mistakes).
- Early notice of problems.
- Easier production of management reports.

(For better reconciliation of corporate transactions two other systems exist for corporates only - FXMatch from Citibank and Concord from CityNetwork).

Whatever the system in force for receiving/sending confirmations, in the event of non-receipt of confirmations, each institution should have an established escalation procedure to follow up missing confirmations, and reports should be despatched to management.

Failure by a counterparty to send confirmation could be the first signal of impending financial failure of that counterparty in that they will not confirm transactions on which they might either lose money or be unable to settle through adverse cash flow, fraud, inefficiency, etc. Although they are no substitute for the actual counterparty confirmation, a Reuters log or interim brokerage note can act as substantiating evidence for both the existence and correctness of a trade (as can taped telephone calls - see page 66 in the Model Code).

A 1999 survey by Benchmarking Technologies International (BTI) in New York emphasised the importance of the back office role in this context. The survey was of 162 US-based corporate and investment clients of 16 major global banks (ranked by Euromoney as amongst the 20 top FX dealers in the world). The two areas most regularly mentioned under 'areas of concern' were 'transparency of pricing' and 'timely, accurate confirmations'. The latter was termed as 'a key service dimension' and the survey found that banks which could not provide confirmation of late trades on trade date were avoided as counterparts. Out of seven areas of performance surveyed, after pricing, quality of service was a close second. Furthermore, respondents were prepared to accept minor pricing differentials provided their risk was managed properly and they received efficient service on confirmations, settlements, inquiries/investigations and ease of doing business.

Cash management

Unless and until you have the answers to the following questions, an efficient management of cash resources/deficits will not be possible.

- When do we know what has happened?
- When do we have to send instructions by?
- What type of instructions have to be sent?
- What are the interest rates on the account?
- What are the market rates?

For even from one nostro holder to another in the same currency the terms for credit/debit balances can vary. The attention to detail in moving money around to maximise income or minimise cost can thus be one means of further enhancing the front office/back office relationship.

The major 'players' in the Treasury market conclude high volumes of transactions - 5,000 plus deals per day per bank are now fairly commonplace in the major financial centres such as London and New York. Where a bank's dealers may not have left a perfectly 'square' overnight position, surplus funds held on nostro accounts together with other 'uncleared' items relating to trade finance instruments which have not yet debited from the nostro accounts, means that funds remain available for investment on overnight deposit.

As banks continue to seek to maximise their revenues, the management and investment of temporarily available cash has grown to be an important function in many back office operations and contributes significantly to the bank's overall profitability. However, in a particularly active institution, many different areas of operation - FX, MM, bonds, futures and swaps - may all generate cash flow, thus a separate section may handle the net position.

By closely monitoring the activity and balances on their accounts, many banks are able to shrewdly invest (usually) overnight these temporarily available surplus funds in the currency's local market thereby earning interest on their deposits. Often successful management of funds depends on fostering good personal relationships with the person(s) responsible for your nostro.

This was especially relevant in the 1970s when both Germany and Switzerland were trying to avoid major revaluations of their currencies.

To effect this, they introduced 'negative' interest rates and imposed a maximum size of balance that any bank could hold on its account (based on average balances over a preceding period). On balances above that figure, large penalties would be imposed. Japan also later imposed something similar by not accepting payments into an account unless it had matching amounts to be paid out.

Even in normal times, the back office staff should keep a close watch on incoming statements from correspondent banks to monitor when overdraft interest rates change. This information should be passed on to not only all the other members of the office but also to dealers so that they are aware of the possible consequences of overdrawing their account.

Naturally, it is essential that all the nostro accounts have first been adequately funded as invariably credit interest rates are lower than overdraft interest rates and an account left overdrawn while 'surplus' funds have been invested will result in a net loss to the bank as the deposit interest earned may not cover any overdraft charges incurred.

Reconciliations

Part of the function of the back office is to reconcile the various accounts used when transacting the treasury business. The reconciliations department is responsible for ensuring that any outstanding amounts are promptly investigated and resolved either by itself or perhaps by its treasury investigations department.

Nostro reconciliations

A nostro account is an account owned by the host bank and maintained with a bank (usually) overseas. The account is denominated in the local currency of the foreign bank and is used by the host bank for settling its treasury business in that particular currency. Therefore, for example, a bank in London which undertakes treasury activity in US dollars will need to open a US dollar account with a bank located in the USA. Each time the host bank in the UK needs to make a payment in USD, it will send an authenticated instruction to its nostro correspondent bank in the USA requesting it to execute the payment. Also, where the bank in London is due to receive a USD payment, it will instruct its counterparty to effect the payment to its nostro account held in the USA.

In order for the nostro bank to be sure that the telegraphic/SWIFT payment instruction which it received from the UK bank is genuine and was sent by the true owner of the account, every payment order has to be authenticated. The process of authentication requires the two banks concerned to exchange 'test keys'. Test keys are secret codes which are known and understood only by the two banks concerned. The construction of the test keys usually involves (in coded format) the amount of the payment order and the date on which it was transmitted by the host bank to its nostro correspondent bank.

Given the fact that anyone who has access to these confidential test keys will have access to the funds in the bank's nostro accounts, it is essential that each bank's test keys are held in a highly secure area usually within its telecommunications department. Also it is vital that the person(s) empowered to effect nostro reconciliation is not also someone who originates transactions - i.e. from front office - or anyone who makes/releases payments. This is obviously necessary to avoid any internal 'wrong-doings' or collusion, (see also page 124.)

Essentially, there are six situations which would explain an unexpected nostro balance:

- A bank expects to receive funds and does not.
- A bank expects to receive funds and receives the wrong amount.
- A bank receives funds and did not expect to receive them.
- A bank expects to pay funds and does not.
- A bank expects to pay funds and pays the wrong amount.
- A bank pays funds and did not expect to pay them.

Nostro statements

In the same way that individual account-holders receive a statement from their bank, showing the balance on their current account, the host banks receive a statement for each nostro account it holds in order that it can check and verify the accuracy of each entry on its account. However, where individuals would normally receive a statement from their bank only monthly, statements on nostro accounts because of the size of the entries and the sheer volume of items, are usually produced and sent by the nostro correspondent on a daily basis (or whenever there is activity/movement over the account).

~ement despatch

If the nostro bank is not a SWIFT user, it will normally send statements to the account holder by mail. However, this method has certain disadvantages as any delay in reconciling the statement can lead to errors taking longer to come to light, and can therefore lead to monetary losses being incurred. Generally, therefore, banks are normally only prepared to accept posted statements where the activity is low to moderate. It is fairly common for such statements to be first sent via fax before the mailed copy is despatched. This enables the account holder to reconcile its account more promptly, thereby allowing earlier notification of possible errors.

The majority of nostro account statements are now sent via the SWIFT network, usually by way of an MT950 or sometimes an MT940. Apart from the high speed at which they can be sent, there is another huge advantage which SWIFT statements have over their mailed versions. Because of the very structured and standardised manner in which SWIFT statements are formatted, they can be electronically downloaded into the host bank's accounting computer system upon receipt. This facilitates the automatic reconciliation (by computer) of many of the entries on the account against the host bank's own internal records of its transactions and therefore reduces considerably the amount of manual (visual) reconciling that needs to be done. In view of the high degree of computerisation, the Model Code recommends that reconciliation be achieved the day after value date.

Book-keeping

Many banks operate what is known as a double-entry book-keeping system. This means simply that each time the host bank makes or is due to receive a payment, a corresponding entry is passed on an internal general ledger account which is associated with the relevant nostro account. Therefore, when funds are expected on a nostro account a general ledger debit is passed internally over the related account. Upon receipt of the funds by the nostro correspondent, the relevant credit will appear on the account. On reconciling the account, the statement credit is reconciled against the ledger debit.

Conversely, upon issuing instructions to the nostro correspondent to execute a payment, the host bank will generate a credit on the related general ledger. Once the nostro bank has made the payment it will debit the host bank's nostro account and this entry will appear on the nostro statement. Once again, upon reconciling the account, the general ledger credit should be matched off against the debit which appears on the statement.

The reconciliations department must ensure that, for each ledger debit and ledger credit that is passed, the nostro account statement should reflect the respective credit and debit in terms of amount, reference (or counterparty) and value date. Failure to correctly reconcile (mismatching) items can lead to an array of problems such as being unaware of valid payments not executed, claiming non-receipt of funds from the wrong counterparty and unwittingly incurring overdraft interest on the nostro account.

As such, absolute vigilance and attention to detail is essential when reconciling the bank's nostro accounts.

Nostro investigations

An outstanding amount on a general ledger or nostro account is often the first indication that a problem exists with a particular transaction. In very broad terms, the following examples illustrate the types of problems which may arise and the reasons why.

- Outstanding ledger debit - may indicate that funds receivable have not been received.

- Outstanding ledger credit - could mean the host bank has failed to execute a payment.

- Outstanding statement credit - may indicate that the host bank has failed to record a deal.

- Outstanding statement debit - could indicate a deal cancelled (in error) or entry passed by nostro bank in error.

The above examples are not definitive but merely show some potential reasons for unreconciled items. Each investigation needs to be handled individually and usually requires reference to the original source document such as the broker's note or Reuters dealing slip. (See Case Study 1, page 175)

CHAPTER 5

III

ANCILLARY RESPONSIBILITIES

Limits/exposure

One of the functions of the deal capture process is to record and update the host bank's records for limit purposes. Each host bank will normally set a maximum trading limit with each counterparty with whom it trades. Individual limits are set in order to monitor the host bank's exposure to each of its dealing counterparties. The host bank's exposure to a particular counterparty reflects the maximum monetary amount which the host bank may lose in the event of that counterparty defaulting on its outstanding deals (owing to insolvency or bankruptcy). It is therefore important that a bank can ascertain on a real-time basis, at any stage during the business day, exactly what its current limit and exposure may be with any one of its trading partners. These limits are usually set based on the counterparty's financial size and strength.

Thus, although the prime responsibility for checking a dealing limit remains with front office, incorrect input - whether by name of bank, geographical location or status - will invalidate many vital reports which are used by management to monitor risk.

Similarly, there is a need for back office staff to understand the implications of incorrect input and to be trained to look out for potential errors, e.g. Deutsche Bank - if a full branch, the limit is fully available, if it is not a full branch, then a subsidiary limit is required; and if the branch is outside the Organisation for Economic Co-operative Development (OECD), then the risk itself and the risk weighting in respect of VaR is very different (see later, page 118).

Dealer's position

Whilst on the face of it, the dealer's position is his responsibility, the back office is instrumental in ensuring that front to back office records agree. Thus it will often be a set procedure that dealers and back office have to agree open positions up to three times per day - at opening, at noon and at close of day. Again, depending on the *modus operandi* of each individual bank and the sophistication of its computer systems, it may be that at this stage of the deal capture process, the dealer's position is updated either automatically or manually.

The dealer's open (currency) position reflects whether that dealer is long (overbought the currency) or short (oversold the currency) or square (neither long nor short - i.e. total purchases match total sales of the currency). An unwanted long or short open position which is held overnight (or overlong intraday) can lead to a monetary loss to the dealer especially in a volatile market where the exchange rate of the currency position being held moves against the dealer in the market.

Dealing Profit and Loss

Two types of Profit and Loss: *Realised* and *Unrealised*

Realised is a result of *squared* position.

Bought/Sold in USD		Rate		JPY Short	JPY Long
Bought	USD 7,500,000	@ 113.10	=	848,250,000	
Sold	USD 5,000,000	@ 113.20	=		566,000,000
Bought	USD 5,000,000	@ 113.15	=	565,750,000	
Sold	USD 5,000,000	@ 113.05	=		565,250,000
Sold	USD 2,500,000	@ 113.45	=		283,625,000
USD Squared		**Realised Profit**		**= JPY 875,000**	

Unrealised is difference between *average rate of position* and *current market rate*

Bought/Sold in USD	Rate	JPY Short	JPY Long
Bought USD 10,000,000	@ 113.00 =	1,130,000,000	
Sold USD 5,000,000	@ 113.08 =		565,400,000
Sold USD 7,500,000	@ 113.10 =		848,250,000
Bought USD 12,000,000	@ 113.05 =	1,356,600,000	
Bought USD 1,000,000	@ 113.02 =	113,020,000	
USD 10,500,000 Long		**JPY 1,185,970,000 Short**	

Average rate is *junior currency amount* divided by *senior currency amount*

Average rate = USD/JPY 112.95

Current market rate = 113.05/10
Unrealised profit calculated as:
(10,500,000 x 113.05) -1,185,970,000
1,187,025,000 - 1,185,970,000 = 1,055,000 JPY

Profit and loss accounting

This step flows from the previous one in that the accurate recording of positions is the first step in assessing profitability. Once the net open position and average rate has been calculated by the system a 'reference' rate can be entered. When compared to a reference rate, the system may be able to determine the profit (or loss) made on each new deal. In today's market, most dealers are paid bonuses based solely on their dealing performance and their profitability to their bank employers. Therefore, dealers will always be very interested in their P&L figures and these may be available to the dealer on demand during the day. P&L statements are also usually produced at the close of business each day/week/month/quarter and at the financial year end. Today, however, in many banks the single input by the dealer automatically updates his position and average rate - thus reliance on back office is reduced.

Depending on the internal policy and control procedures of each bank, the back office may be called upon to verify the accuracy of the dealer's daily

73

P&L figures. This role may also extend to an involvement in full responsibility for revaluation/marking-to-market of your institution's total portfolio.

Here, the main essential is that all rates used are obtained from independent sources, i.e. front office (dealers) are not allowed:

- to supply rates themselves.
- to suggest sources you should use to obtain valuations.
- to receive originals of rates input which in any way could lead to some 'amendment' by them.

Back office staff need to present a strong front in refusing to be induced to depart from the correct procedures. Any undue pressure from front office should be reported to a senior manager (note the importance of separate reporting lines again).

Brokerage

Whereas many banks do conclude Treasury business directly with each other via the telephone, EBS or Reuters, the majority also use - to a degree - brokers as intermediaries. The broker, having successfully brokered a deal between two banks, will charge a commission for bringing the two parties together. The broker will then formally confirm the details of the transaction to both parties by mail, or increasingly now, by electronic means. Both parties are required to check the details stated in the broker's confirmation to ensure the accuracy of the deal and the amount of brokerage charged.

The actual commission or brokerage charged to the banks by the broker will vary according to the currency, the amount, the term (spot or forward) of the deal and whatever commission rates have been agreed individually with each bank. Broker's 'switches' - deals where, due to limit problems, 2 banks need a 3rd party to stand between them (switch) as seller in one deal and buyer in the other - must be clearly distinguished from normal deals via a broker to provide justification for the transaction, an explanation of any different rate of brokerage and form a basis for management reports.

It is normally a function of the back office to not only conduct a daily check of broker's confirmations received (and to investigate and resolve all investigations thereon) but also to receive and check, prior to payment, the broker's monthly invoices/statements (Model Code, page 69 et seq).

Money laundering

Previously, strong competition amongst banks for customer deposits had led to a situation where it was relatively easy for international and local drug dealers to launder the proceeds from drug-trafficking through the banking/financial industry. Many governments have since passed tough legislation requiring the financial industry to advise the police authorities even if they only suspect that an organisation is being used to 'legitimise' any illegally-obtained monies.

All banks have a legal obligation to report any suspicions they may have, and there are penalties for companies who flout the law in this respect. Each bank will have its own method of alerting its staff. In the UK the Bank of England has issued specific instructions - with a video - and members of staff are required to sign to the effect that they have seen and read the relevant material. Furthermore, the Bank of England, at its bi-annual meeting with each bank operating in London, will request confirmation that all existing, and especially new staff have been required to sign accordingly. This is especially relevant where 'bureau de change' activities are undertaken as these are seen as an 'easy target' for access.

Once any suspicion has been notified to the MLRO (money laundering reporting officer), who may or may not refer it on, back office responsibility is fulfilled. The transaction should proceed as normal, since the funds will more likely than not turn up on time, thus it will be up to the police whether they make any attempt to void the transaction or arrest the people behind the transaction. In addition to establishing the procedures for monitoring such sources of funds and educating the staff what to look out for, it is imperative that the MLRO has sufficient status and power to access records when any suspicions are aroused. Otherwise, the unscrupulous depositor will achieve his aim in passing the 3 levels of: placement, layering and integration.

With the creation of the euro, further fears are being expressed about the increased scope for money laundering. This fear has been voiced to the OECD by a special task force which is drawn from 26 governments as well as the European Commission and the Gulf Co-operation Council. The fear is that it will become easier for the criminally-inclined to disguise the origin of funds when a single currency is applied to a series of nations. A euro becomes characterless/unidentifiable when it could emanate from any country - France, Germany, the Netherlands, Luxembourg, Ireland, etc, thereby making the tracking that much more difficult. (Funds from Russia - estimated at some $60 billion - were of especial concern). It will become much easier to change the identity of illegally obtained money so that it appears to have originated from a legitimate source - the point of entry for a euro becomes multiple and quickly becomes anonymous; the exit point can be equally disguised.

Ghost money

The likelihood of the back office being actively involved with 'ghost money' is small, since the initial contact will govern everything and this initial contact would normally be made by senior managers or dealers. Ghost money is the term given to funds which are allegedly available for investment in a large amount for a long-term fixed deposit. Various individuals will turn up with a letter purporting to confirm that they are the legal owners of funds about to mature with another reputable bank. This is evidenced by details on the headed notepaper of this other bank - but if the bank receiving these people is duped into believing this, the 'depositors' will look most reasonable by asking for a small percentage of this deposit as an advance - the deposit, of course, does not exist and the bank loses all the monies advanced.

The only way the back office comes into this is paying the funds mistakenly advanced or in seeking confirmation of the existence of the ghost money. However, strict adherence to procedures in the back office could prevent this type of situation arising. Often the fake deposit has been typed on paper created from the copying of a letter-head tossed thoughtlessly into a waste-paper basket from which a cleaner has retrieved it and passed it on to these fraudsters. Telexes or phone calls may come through to the back office and ask for confirmations of particular deposits - these should not be answered but referred to the head of department, who would need to ensure from instructions already held whether he was in a position to respond to the enquiry. Finally, there have been cases where individuals will phone in purporting to have large sums of money to invest, mostly for long-term deposits or seeking a 'small advance' from a bank prepared to help them in securing much larger amounts. Once again, these calls should not be treated lightly but referred to a higher authority to handle.

Data maintenance/protection

Most banks now take full advantage of the advances in information technology in order to reduce data processing costs and to increase productivity and efficiency in their daily operations. As a result, they depend heavily on the reliability of the various computer systems used across the whole gamut of tasks from accounting to payment execution. Thus, the loss of a bank's computer system will have a major influence on its ability to operate. This is equally true whether the loss is caused by a mechanical failure, power interruption or a computer virus.

For each of these eventualities, a bank should have contingency plans. The usual one would be to export the tapes to an external site so that data can be retrieved in the event of the destruction of records at the bank's address. Similarly, full contingency plans to operate from an external address - should the whole bank be destroyed - were put in place after the Irish Republican Army (IRA) attacks on London and later (unfortunately) in the USA post the events of 11/9/2001.

Internal protection of data is also crucial. It requires the use of individual passwords to access the bank's records. Absences of authorised staff from their desks should only be allowed once access to the screen has been cleared - i.e. they should sign off. Similarly, all employees should be made aware of the requirement not to divulge any information about their employer's business to anyone outside the bank. Indeed, the Data Protection Act specifically requires all people who have access to a database to sign a statement confirming that they will only use the information for the purpose for which it is intended. Any failure to observe these requirements can result in litigation.

The employer is under the obligation to make all such legal/moral compliance requirements clear to employees. Familiarisation with compliance forms is an integral part of back office duties and to remain *au fait* with all changes. A further requirement, under the definition of data maintenance is, that ensuring all automatic systems that generate entries/accounting data based on holidays are regularly updated so that the system does not try to send payments on invalid dates/weekends.

Finally, there is the people problem. The loss of a key member of staff could result in a weakening of control in vital areas - e,g. end-of-year procedures. It could also lead to the weakening of practices in respect of due diligence procedures - i.e. opening accounts, the checking of company Memorandum and Articles to guard against repeats *ultra vires* actions, as in the Hammersmith and Fulham on IRS?

Telephone recording

In view of the vast amounts of money which changes hands daily on the strength of word-of-mouth agreement, it has long been a requirement of the Bank of England that dealing rooms install recording equipment for all dealers' phones. The tapes have to be kept for two months. This practice can easily resolve any dispute on what was or was not said, and is usually extended to back office phones as well. The maintenance of tapes, familiarity with the operation of the machine - especially changes to British Summer Time (BST) from Greenwich Mean Time (GMT) - and security of access (regarding unauthorised alteration/blanking of tapes) all fall within back office duties (page 66 of the Model Code).

CHAPTER 6

|||

POST EMU/THE FUTURE

A survey in April 1998 by Mitchell Madison found that 85% of fund managers think there is a chance of EMU collapsing within the first five years. It is worth remembering that the Maastricht Convention makes absolutely no allowance for any such contingency. (It is also significant that only 53% of the respondents to the survey had any contingency plans themselves!) Possible catalysts might be either a failure in the TARGET settlement system or the effects on the stability of the Euro, brought about by the extension of membership. In the case of the former possibility, what would the ECB do - turn off TARGET and let interest rates float? The major concern is that there is no legal precedent for a currency unsupported by a sovereign state.

What should happen is that the combination of all the nations of EMU, with its new risk-free currency and the impact of technology in a globalised environment, should lead to greater integration of European capital markets. This in turn is expected to lead to an increased level of financial activity in a central exchange risk-free situation which will increase competition, accelerate product development and change institutional and individual behaviour. In the terms of a virtuous circle, this should then lead to a further move in integrating Europe's markets - another survey sees a major repatriation of assets currently held outside the EMU.

If you want to look on the pessimistic side you might consider the following. There are 10,000 banks in Europe today. How many will we need to handle one currency? Also since banks have been dematerialising via derivative market's interest, liquidity and credit risk, will we need any banks at all - or banks as they exist today? Technology is well on the way to replacing them - at least in their current format.

Whatever the outcome, back office will have to make provision for handling payment in euros. 12 countries are now 'in' - Greece having joined late in 2001. Another 14 countries are due to be invited to join Europe, so many more can be expected yet.

Conversion

Over the 1998 May holiday weekend in Britain, it was agreed at political level that the rates at which the participating currencies will be irrevocably locked from 1 January 1999 will be based on their current ERM bilateral central rates. They are set out in Table 6.1. The 'in' national central banks (NCBs) will have ensured, through appropriate market techniques, that on 31 December 1998 market exchange rates between each pair of 'in' currencies - implied by the regular concertation procedure for calculating daily official ECU rates - will equal their ERM bilateral central rates. The treaty requirement that the adoption of the irrevocable conversion rates for the euro must not modify the external value of the ECU (which will be replaced 1:1 by the euro), will thus have been satisfied.

It was not possible to announce before end-1998 the irrevocable conversion rates between each participating currency and the euro itself. This is because the ECU is a currency basket, which includes the Danish krone, the Greek drachma and sterling (which did not participate on 1 January 1999). To calculate the irrevocable conversion rates on 31 December, the regular daily concertation procedure for the official ECU was used (see Fig 6.1).

To convert national currencies into euros, the rates will be expressed to six significant places, for example, euro = FF 6.60054 and euro = DEM 1.96804. Abbreviations to 6.60 or 1.92 are not allowed. Amounts then achieved will be rounded, thus, 2 euro = DEM 3.93608 which becomes 3.94 and 10 euro = DEM 19.6804 which becomes 19.68. Similarly, 100 euro in DEM = 100 x 1.96804 = DEM 196.80 or 100 DEM in euros

Table 6.1 - ERM bilateral central rates used in determining the irrevocable conversion rates for the euro

	DM100=	BF/LF100=	SP100=	FF100=	IEPI=	ITL1000=	DF100=	AS100=	ESC100=	FM100=
DM										
BF/LF	2062.55									
SP	8507.22	412.462								
FF	335.386	16.2608	3.94237							
IEP	40.2676	1.95232	0.473335	12.0063						
ITL	99000.2	4799.90	1163.72	29518.3	2458.56					
DF	112.674	5.46385	1.32445	33.5953	2.79812	1.13812				
AS	703.552	34.1108	8.27006	209.774	17.4719	7.10657	624.415			
ESC	10250.5	496.984	120.492	3056.34	254.560	103.541	9097.53	1456.97		
FM	304.001	14.7391	3.57345	90.6420	7.54951	3.07071	269.806	43.2094	2.96571	

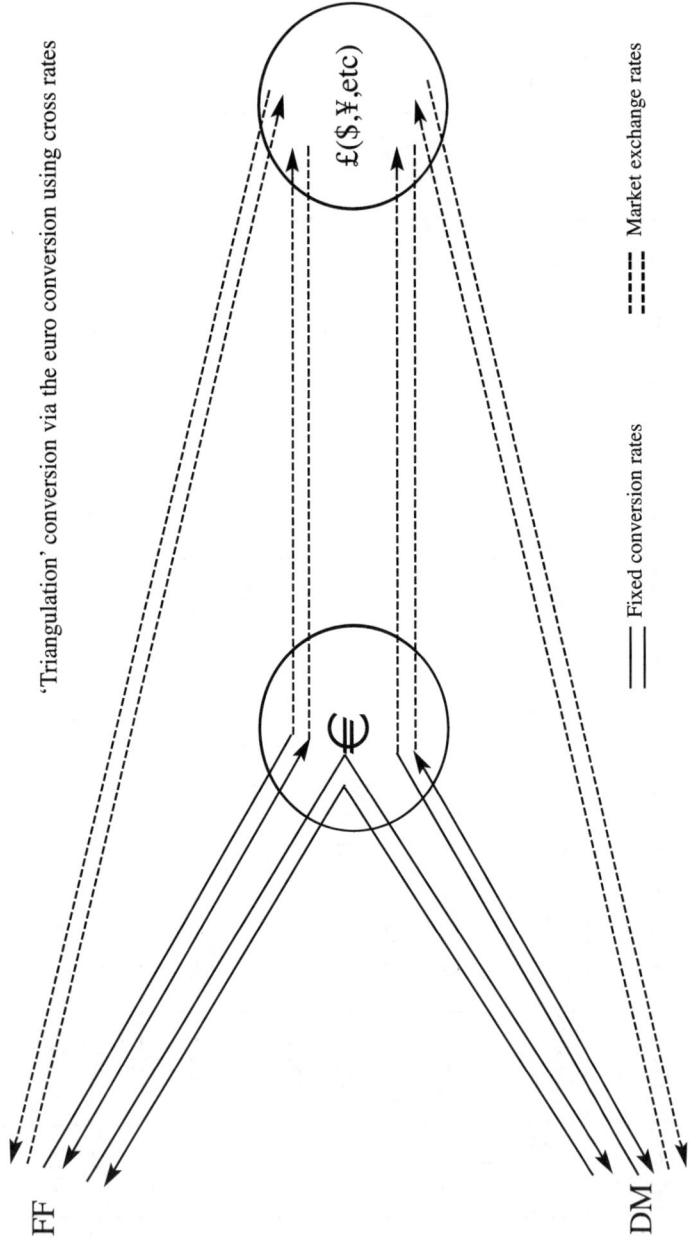

Fig 6.1 Conversion between national denominations of the euro and with other currencies

'Triangulation' conversion via the euro conversion using cross rates

£($,¥,etc)

FF

DM

Fixed conversion rates

Market exchange rates

would be 100/1.96804 = euro 50.811975 = euro 50.81. Inverse rates are not to be used.

Triangulation is used to convert one national currency to another national currency, for example, 10,000 FF converted into DEM would be calculated as follows:

- FF = euro 10,000/ 6.60054 = euro 1,515.0275583.
- Round to euro 1,515.0276.
- Convert into DEM = 1,515.0276 x 1.96804 = DEM 2,981.634917 which gets rounded to 2,981.63.

Converting from 'in' currency to non-participator would be calculated as follows:

If euro = GBP 0.6778 and euro = DEM 1.96804, to convert DEM 1,000 to GBP:

- Convert DEM to euro = 1,000/ 1.96804 = euro 508.119753.
- Convert intermediary amount of euro to GBP = 508.12 x .6778 = GBP 344.40376, which gets rounded to GBP 344.40.

Once all the conversion has been effected, then the euro became just another currency in which to deal. Obviously ahead of the changeover, new accounts in euro had to be established, SSIs exchanged, links to TARGET established, and some training of staff undertaken.

One area which will require some extra attention post-EMU will be that of money laundering. The point of entry for funds emanating from a dubious source will now be much more difficult to track down. Although the various codes of conduct applied around the world make their recommendations regarding the responsibility for checking out sources - i.e. with receiving bank or jointly broker and bank - any suspicion within the back office in respect of a new or unidentifiable depositor is best referred to a compliance officer or money laundering reporting officer so that the back office may rest assured that it has fulfilled its duty.

Post euro

The irrevocable conversion rates between the euro and the 11 participating countries were set on 1 January 1999 (see Table 6.2) + Greece in 2001. The German method of euro conversion of government bonds is rounded up to the nearest cent, thus DEM 100,000 at a conversion rate of E1=DEM 1.92573 becomes E51,928.36. Finland, Luxembourg, Belgium, Ireland, Portugal and Spain will adopt the same method. (Belgium, however, has decided to introduce a new day count basis from 1 January and will not wait till next coupon date).

Table 6.2 - Euro conversion rates

Currency	Euro conversion rate
German marks	1.95583
French francs	6.55957
Italian lire	1936.27
Spanish pesetas	166.386
Dutch guilders	2.29371
Belgian francs	40.3399
Austrian schillings	13.7603
Portuguese escudos	200.482
Finnish markka	5.94573
Irish pounds	0.787564
Luxembourg francs	40.3399
Greek drachmas	340.75

The French method is to round down to the nearest whole euro. Thus FRF 100,000 OAT at a rate of E1=FRF 6.54321 becomes E15,283.00 plus a small cash compensation. The Dutch will round down to the nearest whole euro.

There was some minor disagreement about the GBP and the euro, or vice versa. 80% of the London market met with the Bank of England and the British Banker's Association to agree the EUR/GBP. The EBS reached the same conclusion as the ACI. Eventually, it has settled down as EUR/GBP despite this going against current practice to quote the stronger currency first, and the EUR/GBP would result in a figure less than 1, which proved difficult to master initially but is now accepted.

Swaps

The outcome for capital market transactions - which will require some changes within the back office function - is as follows:

- The fixed leg will be based on an annualised 30/360 day basis.
- The floating leg will be based on six-month Euribor (see below) on an actual/360 day basis.
- The payment date can be any day Monday to Friday except as specified annually by the ECB.
- The fixing date will be any TARGET day two days before start date.

The possibility for change does exist, especially regarding the fixing base. Libor has been a highly effective and respected benchmark for years, and a survey (originated by Westdeutsche Landesbank in London) leaves room for those who were indifferent at the time to come down on the side of Euro Libor after all.

Further question marks relate to the new minimum amounts of trading lots, the disappearance of benchmarks and the method for trading the odd lots created through conversion. ISDA documentation does cater for the failure of new acceptable benchmarks to appear by using quotes provided by specified reference banks.

Euro Libor and Euribor

Euro Libor will be a measure of the cost of euro funds based on the offer rates quoted by 16 of the most active banks in the London market. By contrast, Euribor will be a measure of the average cost of funds over the whole euro area based on a much larger panel of banks (initially 57) and including at least one from each member state within the euro area (see Table 6.3).

Table 6.3 - Alternative Euro Libor settings

	Euro BBA Libor	**Euribor**
Panel	16 major banks active in London	57 banks: 47 selected by national banking associations to represent euro markets in the participating member states. 10 international 'pre-in' banks active in the euro market with an office in the euro area.
Calculation basis	Discard top and bottom 4	Discard top and bottom 15
	Average remainder	Average remainder
Time of fixing	11.00 London time daily	11.00 Brussels time daily
Fixing days	All TARGET days	
For value	Second TARGET day after fixing	
Fixing periods	1 week, 1 month to 12 months	

Many market participants expect there to be a spread between the two rates owing to their different coverage. Euro Libor is likely to be lower than Euribor if ECB reserve requirements impose a cost on deposit-taking by banks established in the euro area. It is possible that the Euro Libor:Euribor spread will be actively traded, for example, using basis swaps.

Use of Euro Libor in the international markets will benefit from familiarity (especially among non-EU institutions), and from the liquidity that derives from the existing weight of contracts based on the current ECU and national currency Libor (which will move over to Euro Libor). In this way Euro Libor will be one of the immediate beneficiaries of EMU; the notional principal of outstanding interest rate swaps in participating currencies in 1995 was some $3,767 billion, second only to US dollar outstandings of $4,372 billion.

International market participants may prefer to link new transactions to Euro Libor in order to avoid the basis risk in relation to wholesale money market positions in London and existing Libor-based assets or liabilities.

Domestic market participants in the euro area, on the other hand, may prefer to use Euribor, which will replace the national interbank rates (Fibor, Pibor, etc) and will use the same panel as the new overnight reference rate for the euro (EONIA). Marché à Terme Internationale de France (MATIF) has announced that it will adopt Euribor. Deutsche Terminbörse (DTB) has announced that it will offer the market a choice, during the transition period, of Euribor and Euro Libor. LIFFE has agreed (January 1999) to use Euribor for its euro contracts.

Euro Libor is available on the basis of T+2, following current British Banker's Association (BBA) market consultations, where T+2 means two TARGET working days after the trade date.

Regulatory changes

The first stage of the reform of financial services regulation was completed in June 1998, when responsibility for banking supervision was transferred to the FSA from the Bank of England. The Financial Services and Markets Act, which received Royal Assent in June 2000 and was implemented on the 1st of December 2001, transferred to the FSA the responsibilities of several other organisations:

- Building Societies Commission.

- Friendly Societies Commission.

- Investment Management Regulatory Organisation.

- Personal Investment Authority.

- Register of Friendly Societies.

- Securities and Futures Authority.

The major concern is that a single body suffers from the same problem as EMU - i.e. the 'one size fits all' theory. A single ombudsman will be addressing all the various problems of the nature of a Barings collapse, the Maxwell scandal, the Roger Levitt case, the various crises at Lloyds of London and the massive pension debacle - although with all that, the size of banking losses over the last 25 years is miniscule in the UK compared to equivalent losses in the USA.

Additionally, it was announced in August 1998 that the capital adequacy requirements, first promulgated by the BIS in 1988, are to be revised. This again will have implications for all the data currently provided via back office for the VaR calculations. New percentages reflecting the relative risk between exposures to an OECD government compared to a normal commercial name are likely to be the major changes.

New instruments

This remains favourite to be the largest source of concern for the back office role. As further mergers take place amongst the financial community, polarising further the level of activity of the top 20/30 banks and the rest, these larger institutions will inevitably put their minds to new ways of trading.

Whilst this would initially only put the onus on the bigger banks' back offices, it will not be long before the other tiers of banks are required by their niche clients to at least account for them if not actively market make in them.

The particular area of rapid expansion at this time is in credit derivatives (see Bank of England Banking Act Report 1996/7, pp. 32/33 and Euromoney, December 1996, pp. 81 et seq), which is a type of insurance offered to protect an exposure just to the risk that the counterparty fails or is sufficiently adversely affected by some occurrence to affect its credit standing. These fall into three categories - the total return swap, the credit spread and the default spread.

CHAPTER 7

███

RISK

We now come to the real implications of the word 'beyond' in this book's title.

Many highly-publicised events - such as the Barings and Orange County fiascos - have given the impression that risk is only associated with derivatives. This is far from the truth. Risk exists in many forms and in varying degrees from deal input to final settlement.

Market risk - see later - starts and remains with the front office (dealers) but most other types of risk are handled, well or badly, by the internal controls put in place and operated by the back office/middle office/audit staff.

Over the last decade, the financial services industry has witnessed substantial growth and significant changes, both internally and externally driven. Some of this change is, indeed, related to increases in derivatives activity.

The bulk of change, however, is attributable to other factors, such as a) the continued evolution of the 'global' marketplace, b) organizational restructurings, c) corporate downsizing,and d) technological developments that permit the streamlining of manual systems and the creation of many new, often complex products (financial engineering).

A recent example of (a) was the evolution in the securities industry via the shortening of some equity settlement cycles - something to be borne in mind as 2002 brought proposed T+1 trading in bonds (now abandoned for a while) from the current T+3. This type of change puts pressure upon existing systems, procedures, and control structures and, needless to say, has been and will continue to be a major challenge.

For (b) we have often witnessed the loss of some safeguards present in one organisation under merger/take over situations, whilst (c) can occur as a result of a cost-cutting exercise leading to the sacrifice of expensive staff. Whilst (d) might lead to an innovation ahead of potential rivals it rarely immediately (if ever) identifies potential problems or the required checks and balances that will be required.

These changes have come rapidly, often without a full understanding or consideration of their effect on systems of internal controls. We are in a state of rapid change where management has often not taken the time to re-examine its traditional control structures and systems to see if they are still relevant and effective.

The internal audit department's/middle office's resources must be focused and re-focused, as changes occur, toward the firm's highest risk areas. By acting thus, we acknowledge that change and risk are correlated - i.e. when there is a major change, such as a re-organization, implementation of a new system, acquisition of a new business, expansion into a new country, introduction of a new product, or passage of new regulations, there is added risk that internal controls will be under stress or inadvertently eliminated.

So What Is Internal Control?

Often - and wrongly - internal control is thought of as the detailed procedures and practices put into place to catch errors and prevent fraud - internal control is much more comprehensive than that. Internal control should be understood as a process by which a company keeps the risks of the business within acceptable bounds - e.g. as interpreted by Central Banks in capital ratio requirements.

The foundation of internal control rests on management's own vision of the importance of controls - as handed down to them by the local regulatory authority.

Risks inherent in the financial services industry include **market risk**,

credit risk and operational risk, which includes all of legal risk, regulatory risk, compliance risk, reputation risk and technology risk. Management must understand the risks before it can effectively manage them.

Each of these risks can be broken down. For example, market risk has several components that relate to movements of prices and interest rates. Market risk also includes liquidity risk (the risk of not being able to unwind a position quickly), basis risk (the risk when different products are used to hedge each other that they may not be sufficiently correlated) etc.

Counterparty risk - relates to credit risk in all its forms - bankruptcy, settlement risk, unauthorised trades - all of which mean you may end up in a creditor's court.

Operational risk consists of traditional concepts, such as authorization to commit a firm's money, protection of assets, complete and accurate recording of transactions, efficient 'due diligence' exercises when opening new relationships, orderly and timely processing and clearance of transactions and reconciliation of individual trade details to a firm's records.

As part of this risk area, technology risk relates to a firm's potential loss of competitiveness in the marketplace due to inadequate technology, both for maintaining the business and servicing customers. Also, technological risk is often associated with the need to protect systems, and the data contained on them, from unauthorized access and tampering.

Internal Control Structure

Once a firm understands its risk appetite, it can build an effective control structure.

Message from the top

This is the first and often the defining level. Without a proper tone from senior management and the board of directors, it would be difficult, perhaps impossible, to set up a good control structure.

Tone at the top is established in several ways - written policies, training programmes and management actions - all of which are necessary to send an accurate message to staff.

Consequent upon the lead set 'from the top', each department or function within an organization must convey a control philosophy that is consistent with overall firm management. Whether it wants to or not, each department sends its own control message - if the manager of a business or support unit does not convey a proper concern for control, neither will his or her staff.

Risk assessment

The second level is risk assessment - understanding a firm's inherent risks and addressing them in relation to the firm's risk tolerance. Then each operating department must 'buy in' to the importance of identifying, evaluating, and managing the risks in its area. This, of course, follows from the tone set at the top - both firm-wide and within each department.

Management information

The third level is management information. Without complete and accurate information about what is going on, it is impossible to be 'in control'. For large, multinational companies, particularly those in the financial services industry, management information is usually one of the most difficult and challenging undertakings because the products, technology, and activity continually change at high speed. Keeping systems up-to-date and able to handle increased volumes of complex transactions, and making sure that they are also properly integrated from a global perspective, is imperative, but often a bit like 'blowing in the wind'.

Control activities

The fourth level concerns control activities. These are the many control procedures and activities that are established to ensure that all business activities are properly authorized, that data is completely and accurately recorded and summarized in the books and records of the company, and that data is properly analysed, periodically reconciled to independent sources, and regularly correlated to expected outcomes. These control procedures and activities comprise the sum total of daily and monthly duties of virtually all employees and are not limited to financial accounting controls.

Monitoring activities

Finally, management needs to establish proper monitoring activities to ensure that its systems of internal control are operating as intended - *'quis custodiet custodes?*' (or who guards the guardians?). Monitoring activities need to permeate the organization, in a helpful not threatening way, and be the eyes and ears of management looking and listening for anything that might go wrong.

The overall message is that monitoring activities must be dynamic enough to adjust to changing environments, yet structured enough to accomplish its objectives.

How to achieve 'best practice' in controlling risk

Promote a learning environment
Get audit/risk managers to talk directly with line-management.

Analyse breakdowns
Find out what went wrong; make suggestions to avoid repetition of errors and identify the control that failed or was missing.

Employ internal auditors from varied disciplines
Ensure there is a varied set of skills present amongst your auditing staff - even some independent deep-thinkers from outside the industry to provide a fresh perspective.

Make control a company-wide responsibility
Each head of department/section must take his/her share of the overall 'tone/message' and the responsibility for activating it.

Illustrating controls

Allegations of lax supervision have been made in the Barings collapse, including suggestions that the trader's supervisors did not understand the products he was trading. An effective review of trading supervision would need to make clear:

a) who manages the trading desk
b) who monitors or supervises the traders
c) whether the supervisor understands the transactions being conducted
d) whether the supervisor has been properly instructed and indoctrinated into the firm's culture and the importance it places on controls and risk management
e) who the supervisor reports to

f) whether risk reports are prepared

g) whether there are adequate controls to ensure the risk reports are accurate

h) whether the firm has a chief risk manager, or risk management committee, or both

i) whether those people assume an oversight function

As you can see, these are the same questions that surface whether you are dealing in derivatives or any other product.

The Cost of Control

There can be a problem when it comes to assessing the cost of control, but if control is handled properly, cost should not be a major factor in the equation. Effective control does not mean adding a major separate infrastructure. The key is creating a culture of awareness throughout the company. Then, there will be less need to double-check and audit the transactions. Obviously, you can never completely eradicate the need to audit and provide assurance, but if you invest in an effective control structure, there will be fewer controversies with customers, other firms, and regulators - and controversies often attract sizeable costs.

As emphasised throughout this book, with the best will in the world, the roles carried out by the back office itself could be the source of some of the eventual risk that is being run by any institution. This comes under the category of operational risk. So what we need to examine further are what constitutes operational risk beyond that which we have so far explored.

Operational/technological risk

This risk encompasses everything that can go wrong with the processing procedure. Our reliance on technology is absolute. If one follows the chain of processing systems through the cycle it becomes apparent that not only is there a myriad of systems controlling the reporting and processing function within your own organisations, but also that banks are reliant on international clearing and payment systems - i.e. CHIPS and CHAPS, and the processing systems of your counterparty. Add in external information providers, such as Reuters and Bloomberg, and regulatory reporting systems, such as TRAX, and it becomes very apparent that banks, particularly trading rooms, are driven by technology and also the need to remain state of the art.

System failure is now the great concern of banks. It is no longer acceptable or possible to treat long-term loss of functionality as something that can be sorted out at the home of the general manager or head trader. Contingency planning has become big business. Terrorism and incidents like the hurricane of 1987 have focused the attention of financial institutions. All systems must be fully backed up, duplicated and, if possible, be available immediately in the event of a disaster. Banks now plan on the loss of premises through terrorism, fire, etc., and how quickly they can get back into full business from nothing. The aim is under 48 hours.

At the other end of the spectrum is human error. Whilst systems are designed to help the user in automating many of the repetitions in processing, there always remains the risk that incorrect payment instructions or mis-keying leads to interest penalty claims. Operational managers are now beginning to implement controls based on performance levels (benchmarking) that help identify the weaknesses in processing systems. Operations departments are being asked to sign service level agreements with their respective front offices.

Some factors which impact on risk management are outside the direct control of the institution itself or its back office. Most of that risk is down to external influences. Of these the major risk, both in terms of likelihood and actual impact, is settlement risk (see Fig 7.1).

Settlement risk

How can one define settlement risk? In the course of business there will come a specific date, as defined by the relevant contract, where Counterparty A must pay Counterparty B in settlement of a transaction. It is the receiving party that takes the risk of non-receipt. If he does not receive payment then he is out of pocket for the full amount of the payment or 100% of the nominal value of the contract or the agreed margin in the case of a derivative contract. This is called the credit risk dimension of settlement risk.

Instrument types that incur counterparty settlement risk at maturity include:

- FX spot - each counterparty will be expecting settlement from each other.
- Maturing FX forward contracts - becomes a spot contract two days prior to maturity.

Fig 7.1 - Today's trading process - where's the risk?

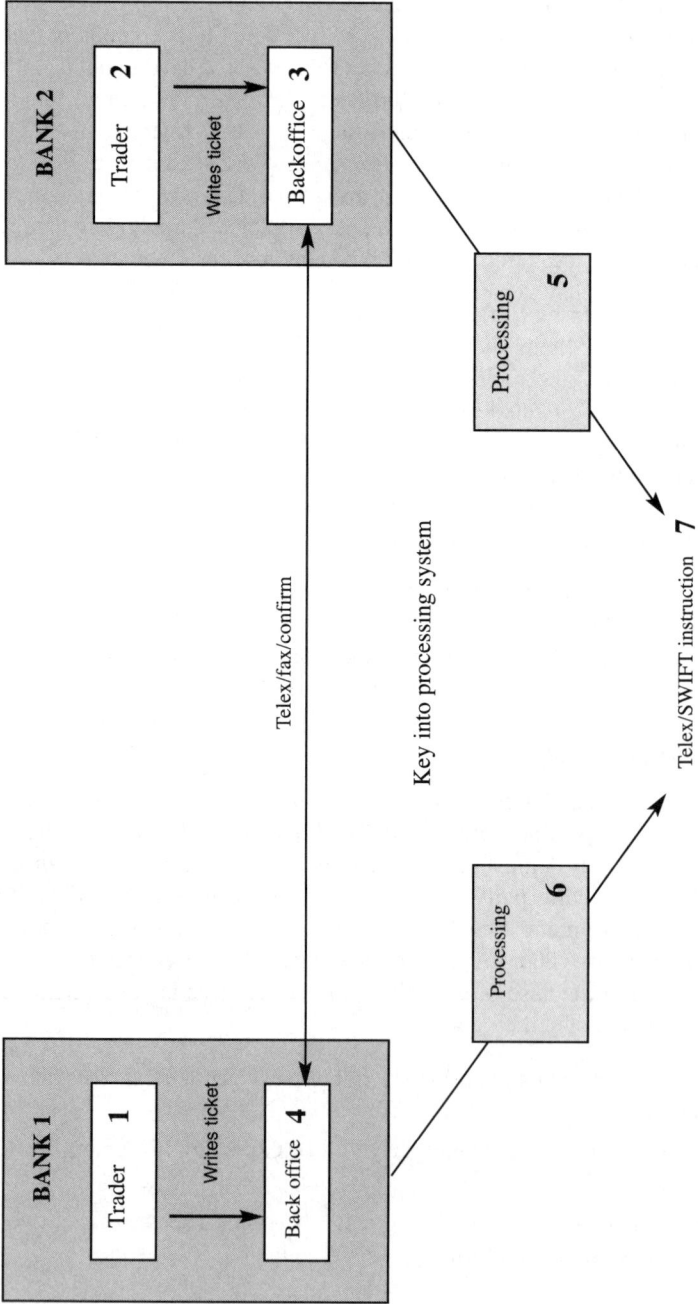

- Any free Eurobond settlement - i.e. between different custodians or nostros (not Euroclear and Clearstream).

- The payment of margin or fees in relation to futures contracts or FRAs.

- Option premiums.

- Transfers of payment on interest rate or currency swaps.

Whilst we consider the counterparty, and set limits that reflect the total amount of payments to be received on any particular day from him, by far the majority of non-receipt of funds are owing to human/system errors. They typically represent:

1. Dealers inputting incorrect details on the ticket
2. System failure
3. Incorrect checking of confirmations by back office

Page 52 of the the Model Code, identifies 1. and 3. as the major causes of error.

The aspect of most concern in settlement risk, particularly in the FX market, is the risk of releasing payment before confirmation of receipt of the incoming funds has been received. Think of the UK bank who has sold yen against US dollars. To make payment in yen he will have to release his payment instruction two days prior to the settlement date. Japan is closed as the UK opens for same value, and the banks require the payment instructions the day before settlement. The US dollar receipt will not be advised until the morning after the settlement date. The US closes at 8 pm UK time, when hopefully most of us have gone home. Settlement risk is also known as Herstatt risk (see page 40 and Fig 7.2).

Settlement exposure

Limits set for settlement are usually called daily settlement lines (DSLs). They reflect the total amount to be settled between counterparties on one business day. The limit applied will reflect the volume of business undertaken with a particular counterparty and include any bilateral or multilateral netting agreements in place.

Fig 7.2 - Cross currency settlement risk (Herstatt, 1974)

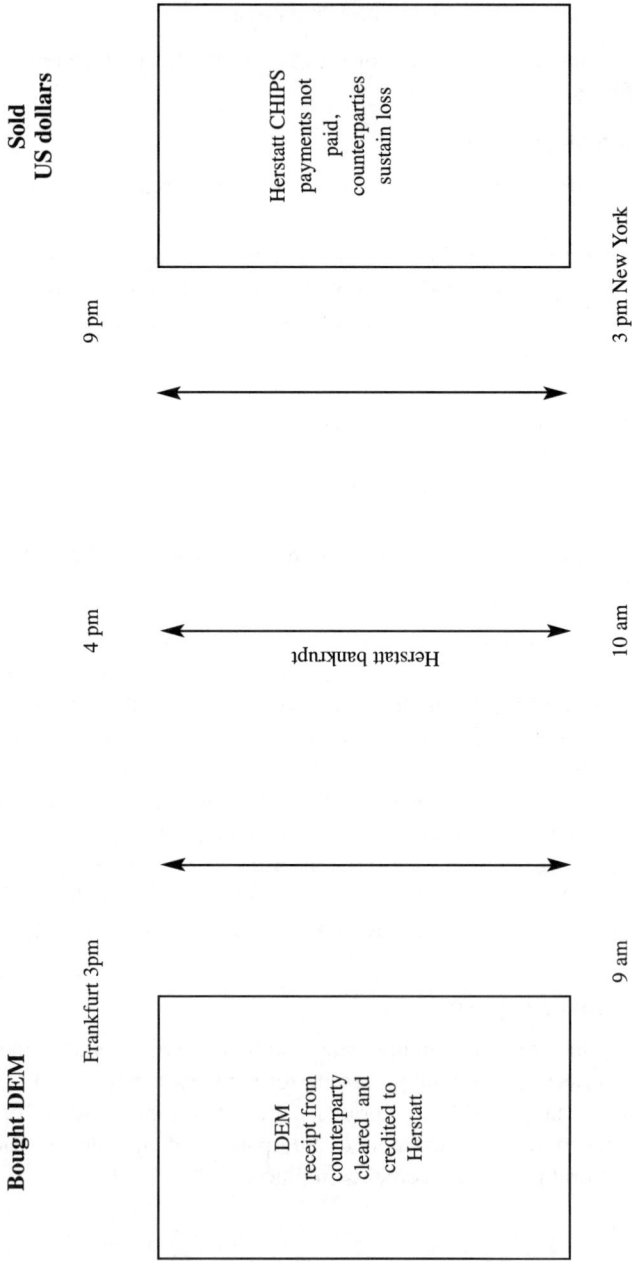

Bought DEM

**Sold
US dollars**

Frankfurt 3pm	4 pm	9 pm	
	Herstatt bankrupt		3 pm New York
9 am	10 am		

DEM
receipt from
counterparty
cleared and
credited to
Herstatt

Herstatt CHIPS
payments not
paid,
counterparties
sustain loss

The more sophisticated the system, the more accurate the limits. The limits can be multi-product - after all settlement of cash is the same regardless of the product - however this assumes that settlements from many different systems can be amalgamated under one limit.

The Committee on Payment and Settlement Systems (CPSS) of the G10 Central Banks has advanced a case for assessing settlement risk to be equal in aggregate to a multiple of the average daily FX turnover figure reported by the BIS. It even thinks that a bank's maximum FX/settlement exposure could equal or even surpass the amount receivable for three day's worth of trades. This could amount to a figure for any one counterparty which exceeds the bank's entire capital.

The collapses of the US investment bank, Drexel Burnham Lambert, in 1990, BCCI in 1991 and Barings in 1995 are excellent case studies for this type of risk. The amount at risk equals the full amount of currency purchased and lasts from the time that a payment currency (for the currency sold) can no longer be cancelled unilaterally until the time the currency purchased is received with finality (irrevocable and unconditional).

The Noel Report of 1993 assumes the fundamental concept that multi-currency DVP is assured. This means that the final transfer of one asset only occurs if, and only if, the final transfer of another asset occurs.

In June 1998 the SWIFT US National Group released a set of recommendations to improve market practices in respect of cancellations and reconciliations of FX transaction thereby reducing interbank settlement exposure and decreasing FX settlement risk. The report suggested that the required reduction in risk profile can be achieved through improvements to back office processing, correspondent banking arrangements, netting capabilities and risk management controls. Thus it should be anticipated that the back office will have new and additional demands made of it in the coming months/years.

One way is to secure the agreement on an industry level by setting rules and creating service level agreements for FX nostro banks. This was formalised in April 1998 under a paper called RISE. This report recommends that:

- The cancellation deadline should be no more than two hours before the corresponding clearing system's opening.

- All credit advice messages should be sent within 10 minutes of receipt of the credit from CHIPS, Fedwire or other clearing systems.

- Beneficiary banks should have the ability to reconcile within two hours of the closing time.

- Final reconciliation should be within 30 minutes of the closing time of the latest local payments system.

- Banks using MT 210s should reconcile within two hours of the closing time.

- Banks should use SSIs as a default.

Whilst a considerable number of the decisions on the above will be individual choices, any changes will - once again - end up as back office primary responsibilities.

The authorities are also concerned with systemic and liquidity risk. Liquidity risk envisages the scenario where the availability of a currency or instrument becomes nil or there is no longer a market and settlement cannot be made. Examples of this situation include currencies becoming non-convertible.

Systemic risk is where there is a concern that the inability of a financial institution to make payment or settle a contract will cause its counterparty to fail, and there becomes a knock-on effect throughout the international markets.

Other external sources of risk - again totally outside any individual institution's control - are limited to:

Legal risk

Whilst this includes documentation and the risk of claims made against a defaulting client through the courts, it also includes the legal status of companies/corporates and their power to enter into various types of transactions. Hammersmith & Fulham Borough was deemed to have illegally entered into derivative transactions. As a result, consequently banks were unable to claim against the authority for losses made, as H&M had conducted transactions outside its powers (ultra vires).

The regulatory structure in the UK - ultimately the FSA - sets strict rules in relation to how business is to be undertaken. It is each bank's responsibility to ensure that it has in place procedures that ensure sensitive information is managed responsibly on a need to know basis - i.e. 'due diligence' is correctly carried out so that banks truly 'know their customer', as specified on page 31 in the Model Code.

Political risk

In some parts of the world the instability of the political regime causes concern. The fact that governments can, through policy and military take-overs, effectively change the business structure of a country and directly cause losses to existing positions and/or portfolios is a clear risk. Banks will set country limits, which control the level of exposure they are prepared to take in a particular country. It is likely that the USA or G7 type economies will have unlimited exposure, yet some of the African countries can not even be described as emerging. It is unlikely that banks will want to engage in high levels of exposure in these types of countries. For this reason banks set regional and global limits in addition to individual counterparty limits.

Adverse publicity risk

Financial institutions hate bad publicity. It can, in the worst case, bring a company to its knees. Irving Trust was a US bank that sacked one of its employees from the IT department. This person promptly hacked back into Irving's money transfer system. He did not steal money, but instead made public what he had done. Customers were extremely concerned about this lack of security and promptly moved their accounts to another bank.

In 1998, the Asian currency crisis was reflected in some good name Western banks which had large exposures in the region, either as a source of profit or as a region where they had many clients, suffering a run on deposits and/or credit rating mark-downs.

Fraud

Financial institutions also need to protect themselves from fraud both internally and externally. International action through the Financial Action Task Force (a committee set up by 26 member countries) continues the war against money launderers. Banks need to be vigilant for fraudulent or counterfeit documents presented for payment. Another very common type of fraud is through internal theft and is usually for relatively small amounts.

This does not exhaust the total sources of risk. In fact it leaves the major one that applies to all front office operations - market risk. Even though back office does not create market risk or assume prime responsibility for its monitoring, many of the controls that can be exercised to educe/monitor/minimise it will often fall within the duties of some part of the 'support' or back office function. It is a very real risk and one which, with the appropriate level of co-operation and care between all interested parties, can be actively managed and kept within bounds.

Market risk

Market risk involves determining the sensitivity of a currency/instrument to changes in the financial markets and assessing the extent of the exposure to the risks of such changes. The risk must be measured across the entire portfolio of currencies and instruments. Given the size and diversity of some investment banks' trading portfolios, this is not an inconsiderable task. Let's look firstly at foreign exchange and where the risks derive.

FX spot

Currency mismatching of one currency varies in value against another. All convertible currencies are valued against the US$ (world trade is conducted in US$). The calculation of cross rates are worked through the dollar equivalent of both currencies. The value of one currency may therefore change in relation to the US$ owing to economic pressures or political influences that are specific to that currency.

The price at which each currency is bought or held will inevitably change throughout the day and certainly overnight as it is traded internationally and has no respect for time zones. A client places a large order with a bank, which is accepted. In an extreme case the order may mean that the FX spot desk is holding a very large position (long or short) until it has managed to cover the position in the market. Large buyers or sellers can change the market price. It is likely that the position can only be offloaded in bits. It is conceivable that the price may move against the original cost of the order whilst the bank goes about clearing the position. The head trader must have been aware of this intraday risk and factored this into his or her decision to accept the order.

Overnight risk reflects any price movement against the average price of any net position held overnight. In the morning the trader could arrive to see adverse movements in rates internationally that have altered the current value of his position.

FX forwards

Movements in forward foreign exchange rates are dictated by movements in relative interest rates. Forward rates are calculated using the respective interest rate for that currency for like periods. Consequently a six-month forward CHF price and the six-month USD interbank will reflect the six-month CHF interbank rates in the same market place. It therefore follows that any change in interest rates will have an impact on the forward price. Forward positions therefore are subject not only to currency risks but also to interest rate risk (see page 104).

In setting realistic trading limits for forwards, it is essential to have an accurate method of quantifying the level of risk (the worst case loss) in the event of extreme price fluctuations. The risk is normally expressed as a percentage of a currency position and limits are set accordingly. Because US dollars are viewed as a relatively stable currency, a larger forward position than say a forward position in Argentinean pesos which is a more volatile currency, may be allowed. The limits and level of risk to be taken will always be judgemental; what counts is accurately identifying and measuring the risk (see value at risk, on page 118).

It is worth saying something about arbitrage. On occasions there may arise an interest rate differential between currencies that does not accurately reflect the respective forward prices. In other words, purchasing another currency forward may be advantageous because the cost of converting may be cheaper or the interest rate cost less. Identifying any such trading opportunities is called arbitrage. In an efficient market these windows of opportunity do not last long. Market forces will bring the rates into line and the window will close.

Interest rate risk

Interest rate risk can be defined as the exposure of a bank's financial condition to adverse changes in interest rates. As an excessive interest rate risk can be a significant threat to the bank's earnings and capital base, sound risk management systems are required. Limits need to be realistic and the methodology of calculating risk accurate in order for exposure to be kept within realistic levels.

Gap risk/repricing risk

This is the most widely understood type of interest rate risk. It arises from timing differences in maturities and the repricing process.

The example used in Chapter 1 to describe risk diversification can also be used to identify the unhedged risk created by funding a fixed rate loan against short-term deposit on a repricing basis.

A US$10m bank loan for one year at 6% is funded by a three-month deposit at 5.5%. If, at the end of three months, interest rates have risen to say 6.5% the margin has moved from a profitable situation to one that will post losses to the P&L. The cash flows on the loan are fixed over its lifetime, while interest paid on the funding is variable and, in this example, has increased after the short-term deposit matures.

Yield curve risk

What does the yield curve represent? It reflects the economic value of interest rate instruments which include bonds and the money markets. The economic value can be defined as the current value of future cash flows. A 10-year fixed rate bond halfway through its term is unlikely to be valued at par owing to rate changes since inception, the shortened maturity profile, and the remaining coupon payments. The yield curve therefore reflects the time value of money. The classic yield curve shape shows short-term rates lower than long-term rates in a gradual arc upwards over time. On occasions the curve can become flat (where short-term rates and long-term rates are the same) or inverted (where short-term rates are higher than long-term rates). Usually for curves to become flat or inverted, local government monetary policy is influencing the market.

Yield curve risk occurs when anticipated shifts of the yield curve have adverse effects on a bank's income or underlying economic value. For instance, the economic value in a short position in 10-year government bonds hedged by a long position in 5-year government notes could decline sharply if the yield curve steepens, even if the position is hedged against parallel movements in the yield curve.

We have seen the relationship between the FX forward rate and interest rates. Whilst the changes in value between different currencies have an impact on the forward rate, changes in interest rates also have an impact through mismatched positions and yield curve risk. Other related products that are influenced by interest rate risk are forward rate agreements (which are hedging instruments), interest rate futures and interest rate swaps.

Basis risk

Another important source of risk arises from the imperfect correlation in the adjustment of rates earned and paid on different instruments with otherwise similar repricing characteristics. Cash (or the underlying) markets may not move at the same speed as a derivative. For example, if a one-year loan that is renewed monthly based on Libor is hedged by a deposit that reprices monthly but is based on the US treasury bill rate, there may be spread changes as the two index rates move closer or apart.

Liquidity risk

Liquidity risk arises where, for whatever reason - lack of players, economic crises, war etc. - a price is either not available in the currency/instruments required, or not available in any size. The way to avoid such problems is to deal only in those currencies and instruments which always have deep liquidity.

Correlation risk

This reflects the risk emanating from instruments that can be matched through similar or opposite price correlations, and can be used as an offset against each other. They need not be of similar repricing or market types. For example, the US$/DEM rate had similar price characteristics as the US$/NLG (Netherlands guilders) as both currencies were economically tied through the ERM. As both rates will tend to move in the same direction it is noted that the rates are positively correlated and a long position in one currency will be offset by a short position in the other.

Equally in some instances the price movement of a currency or instrument may be matched by an instrument that moves in the opposite way. This is known as negative correlation and therefore two long positions can be offset against each other. If there is no correlation between rates either positively or negatively, then no offset can be achieved. This is called nil correlation.

Replacement risk

This represents the maximum a bank/institution might lose when called upon to go back to the market and replace a deal at current prevailing rates and comparing that to the rate on the original deal.

Let's look at an example:

*   We buy GBP 1,000,000 @ 1.65 for USD 1,650,000 value 6 months. After 3 months, the client goes bankrupt (3-month forward FX rates are @ 1.75).

*   Replacement cost of contract: GBP 1,000,000 will cost USD 1,750,000.

*   Result: If the customer cannot deliver and defaults on the contract we must cover our new exposure on the market at a potential loss of USD 100,000.

If your counterparty declares bankruptcy before the settlement of forward or off balance sheet type transactions then, assuming a hedged position, the transaction must be replaced in the market. It is unlikely that this can be done at the existing rate as rates will have changed and you will need to replace the transaction for a shorter period than the original contract. The risk is that the rates will have moved adversely and there is a loss to book. As in all cases of risk measurement, you must assume worst case.

Firstly it becomes apparent that replacement is measured against the individual transaction and not against a portfolio of trades that is the case with market risk. With each counterparty it is possible to have facilities for several product types, e.g. FX spot (or settlement limits), FX forwards, interbank loans, IRS and fixed income trading. Each product type will be measured and analysed against historical volatility models.

To better understand how this (and all the other risks we have identified) can be controlled, we need to proceed to the next chapter - risk management.

CHAPTER 8

▐▐▐

RISK MANAGEMENT

Although risk is always initiated by the front office, the back office (or maybe middle office) will to a large extent, be instrumental in the process of managing risk. Many of the duties that have been covered in the earlier chapters will - provided they are carried out efficiently - lessen the risk profile. However, in most instances the back office will only be involved after the risk has already been assumed. It is on front office risk that we will now concentrate.

As touched upon earlier, although it would be theoretically possible for additional external controls to be implemented to control risk, however, the cost, intrusiveness and difficulty in gaining acceptance can make it impractical after all. However, there is a logic that says that central authorities should set the ground rules on which internal controls are used.

Major losses resulting from poor quality loans both by sector and geographical location led to the establishment of the Cooke Committee which eventually brought out the 8% capital requirement in 1987. Since that time, other market losses have led the central authorities to extend their recommendations beyond those of the maintenance of the statutory 8% capital to the requirement to risk - weight and correlate the whole portfolio of an institution to arrive at the concept of the maximum risk reflected in one number - VaR - value at risk.

Recent developments

On the basis of the crises that arose in Asia (1998), leading central banks - led by the US Federal Reserve - raised concerns concerning the IMF's proposal to set its own 'code of conduct'. The main objection is that the IMF draft rules seem to be set to suit itself, whilst an additional concern was that, extending these rules to cover payment systems, was seen as going too far. In the event, the IMF code produced an 8-point benchmark plan which individual central banks were allowed to interpret within their own sphere of influence.

The IMF has no power to enforce this code of conduct, it tends instead to use 'peer presure' when necessary. It does have the power over those countries to whom it makes loans, imposing conditions on these loans and sanctions in the event of a default.

This concern is not confined to the IMF document. In the UK, the City has expressed major reservations about the scope of the new Financial Services Authority. Concerns were expressed on such matters as accountability, appeals procedures, the definition of market abuse and the need to distinguish between retail and wholesale markets.

The main area was the definition of market abuse. This needs clarification regarding the description of market abuse concerning situations when:

a) artificial transactions give the market the wrong impression of supply and demand market squeezes.

b) where a single player temporarily controls an instrument and thus its price.

c) the use of privileged information

The FSA handbook specifically covers this under section 1 of MAR 1-4

Whilst the initial decision would be taken by the front office, there would be a natural spin-off for the back office to draw the attention of senior management - via its separate reporting line - of any 'unsual' practices.

Accountants have also took fright at the results of the Asian crisis moved to using 'International Accounting Standards'. Specific matters covered would be:

- Related party lending and borrowing
- Losses arising from foreign currency debt
- Derivative financial instruments
- Reporting by financial sector
- Contingent liabilities

110

A recent report showed that, of 73 banks surveyed in Korea, Thailand, Indonesia, Malaysia and the Philippines, only 25% disclose 'receivables' from associate companies; only 34% reported inter-company loans and deposits; none declared the company's risk management policy; just 19% declared foreign currency profit and losses accurately; 1% only disclosed their risks associated with derivatives and less than a third of all companies described their business by market sector.

The relevance of any new demands here on back office would be extra vigilance required on counterparties in any of these geographical areas regarding confirmations, changes in activity or acceptance of non-market pricing or additional exposure created by the front office itself to counterparties in this region.

Payment Netting

This is one of the most effective ways of reducing settlement risk between trading counterparties. Payment netting is defined as the arrangement between two counterparties to net all payments in a single currency owed between them on a given value date. The payments will be aggregated to arrive at a single currency obligation for each currency payable between the parties. The parties calculate net payments at an agreed time (usually the day before value).

Netting of payments between two counterparties (most actively used between counterparties in foreign exchange markets but can be used for many products where payments are to be made in the same currency) is known as bilateral settlement netting.

Bilateral netting

Netting arrangements are encouraged by the central authorities and have an obvious benefit to those parties involved - i.e.

- The number of payments in progress and volume in transit is dramatically reduced.
- The opportunity for errors is reduced as 'human' error is largely excluded.
- Reconciliation is easier.
- Charges, when incurred, are likely to be smaller.

Against that, one has to weigh the cost of the initial set-up of netting - hardware and software - and recognise that the mere agreement of a net position between counterparties does not totally eliminate risk. For there

111

is no guarantee that netted payments by both parties will be simultaneous, thus delivery risk may still apply.

How in practice would the various netting systems work? What is their practical application? Netting can occur on a bilateral basis - i.e. between the offices of two banks only - or on a multilateral basis - i.e. where branches of more than 2 banks settle on a net basis.

Example: Bank A is due to make 5 payments totalling CHF 10M to Bank B. Bank B is due to make 4 payments to Bank A totalling CHF 5M. Instead of the two banks making a total of 9 payments, Bank A would simply make 1 payment to Bank B for CHF 5M with one net payment of the counter-currency (this could be in either direction depending on the FX rates that applied).

Bilateral netting results in one net payment, per currency, per counterparty, per day.

Multilateral netting

Multilateral netting is a group of banks agreeing to net their payment obligations. For example:

> Bank A buys DEM 100, sells USD 99 with Bank B.
> Bank A sells DEM 85, buys USD 85 with Bank C.
> Bank B buys DEM 75 and sells USD 74 with Bank C.

The effect on each bank's positions is shown in Table 8.1.

In this example Banks A, B and C do one trade with each other which, with a bilateral arrangement, would leave settlement unchanged from a gross position. On a multilateral basis, however, when banks can net across all their counterparties the resulting positions are lower. Here the total payments under a bilateral netting arrangement would total USD 516, under a multilateral arrangement the figure is reduced to USD 50.

Multilateral netting results in one net payment per currency per day.

Legal documentation

The most widely used and internationally accepted form of documentation is the ISDA master agreement. ISDA, International Swap & Derivative Association Inc, (see Fig 8.1) supports a bilateral agreement for settlement in the following products:

- Interest rate and currency swaps
- Foreign exchange settlement
- The exercising of OTC options including currency options

112

Table 8.1 - A multilateral position

Trades and Positions	Bank A DEM	USD	Bank B DEM	USD	Bank C DEM	USD
Example trades						
1.	100	(99)	(100)	99		
2.	(85)	85			85	(85)
3.			75	(74)	(75)	74
Notional bilateral positions vs. counterparty						
Bank A. (85)			(100)	99		85
Bank B.	100	(99)			75	(74)
Bank C.	(85)	85	(75)	74		
Multilateral positions	15	(14)	(25)	25	10	(11)

The agreement allows for early termination and close-out netting. The agreement is binding and supported internationally. It is accepted by all major banks operating in the underlying and derivative markets.

Fig 8.1 - 1992 ISDA documentation architecture

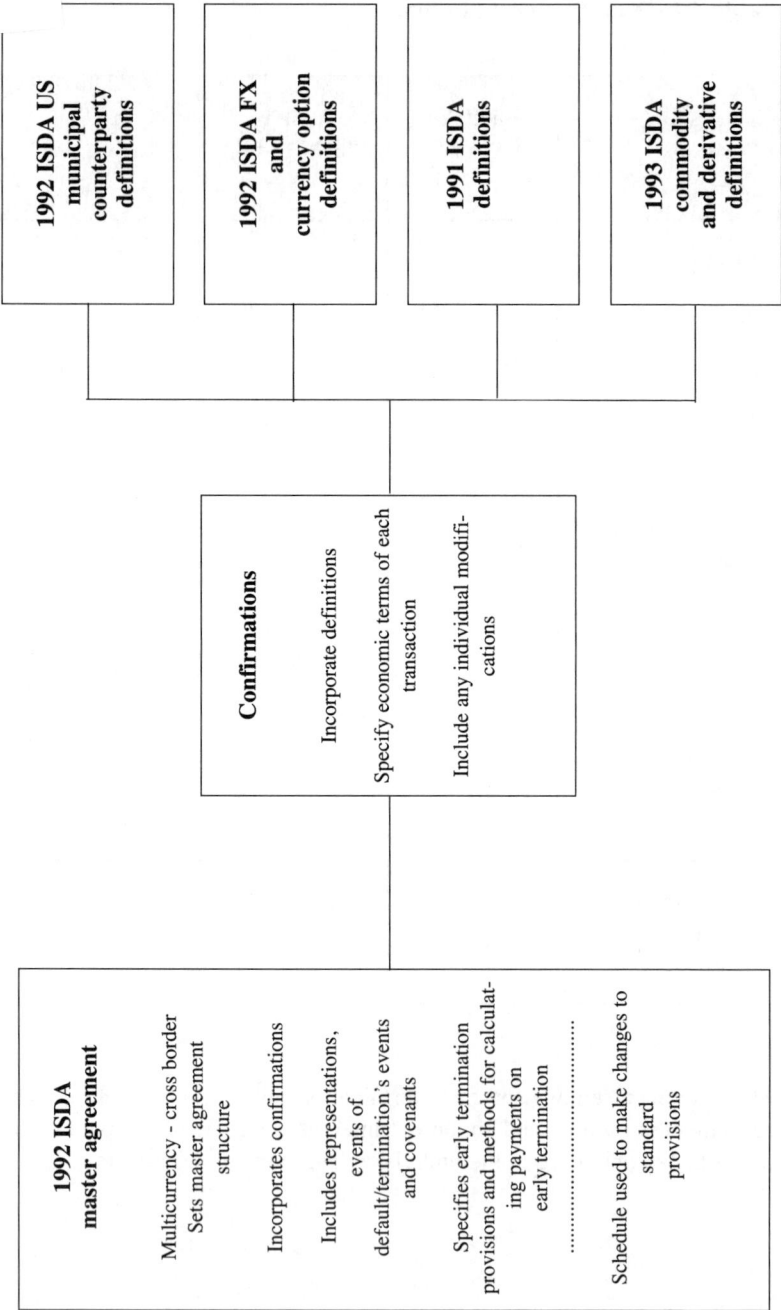

```
┌─────────────────────┐
│ 1992 ISDA US         │
│ municipal            │
│ counterparty         │
│ definitions          │
└─────────────────────┘

┌─────────────────────┐
│ 1992 ISDA FX         │
│ and                  │
│ currency option      │
│ definitions          │
└─────────────────────┘

┌─────────────────────┐
│ 1991 ISDA            │
│ definitions          │
└─────────────────────┘

┌─────────────────────┐
│ 1993 ISDA            │
│ commodity            │
│ and derivative       │
│ definitions          │
└─────────────────────┘
```

Confirmations

Incorporate definitions

Specify economic terms of each transaction

Include any individual modifications

1992 ISDA master agreement

Multicurrency - cross border
Sets master agreement structure

Incorporates confirmations

Includes representations, events of default/termination's events and covenants

Specifies early termination provisions and methods for calculating payments on early termination
....
Schedule used to make changes to standard provisions

Netting by novation

Novation netting is arranged when a contract is entered into and not at settlement. Novation netting entails that for each value date and for each currency the parties agree that all existing contracts will be cancelled and simultaneously replaced by a new, legally-binding contract that aggregates and nets all of the payment obligations of the previous contracts. In circumstances that involve bankruptcy, novation removes selective settlement (so-called 'cherry-picking') by the liquidator of the bankrupt company, i.e. settling the most profitable contracts.

On settlement date, however, no difference exists between the amounts that would be calculated under novation versus the amounts calculated under payment netting. What it adds is greater security for the non-defaulting party. Thus, we arrive at close-out netting - the methodology used to work out net amount receivable/payable.

Close-out netting

This form of netting is effectively a credit risk management tool in the event of default by a party to a trading contract. In this case the non-defaulting party has the legal right to liquidate and set off all outstanding transactions between parties. The terms of close-out are agreed between the parties including the timing and pricing methodology. Close-out netting is the calculation of the replacement cost of each transaction to the non-defaulting counterparty, converted to an agreed single currency and netted.

Let's look at an example:

Contract 1
ABC Bank buys USD 5 million against CHF 7,303,000, value 5 September at 1.4606 with XYZ Bank.

Contract 2
ABC Bank sells JPY 1 billion against USD 10,277,492, value 18 September at 97.3 with XYZ Bank.

Contract 3
ABC Bank buys USD 5 million against CAD 5,990,000, value 3 October at 1.1980 with XYZ Bank.

Contract 4
ABC Bank buys GBP 5 million against USD 7,763000, value 6 October at 1.5526 with XYZ Bank.

Let's assume that XYZ Bank defaults on 3 September, before these contracts mature. ABC Bank under the terms of its contract with XYZ Bank can calculate the replacement cost of the above contracts. The replacement value is defined as the amount that would have to be paid to enter into a contract having the same economic value as the original contract. ABC has to enter into contracts that are equal and offsetting to the original contracts for the same value dates as the original contracts.

Contract 1

The CHF has appreciated against the USD to 1.43. ABC will need to sell CHF 7,150,000 new counterparty to buy back USD 5 million, making a profit.

CHF	7,303,000		
	- 7,150,000		
CHF	153,000/1.43	=	USD 106,993

Contract 2

The JPY has appreciated to 96.5 which, when sold at this rate realises USD 10,362,694, another profit.

USD	-10,277,492
	+10,362,694
USD	+ 85,202

Contract 3

The Canadian dollar has appreciated against the USD to 1.17. ABC will now need to sell CAD 5,850,000 to buy back USD 5 million.

CAD	5,990,000		
	- 5,850,000		
CAD	140,000/1.17	=	+USD 119,658

Contract 4

GBP has appreciated against the USD to 1.57. ABC will now need to sell USD 7,850,000 to buy back GBP 5 million.

US	7,763,000
	- 7,850,000
US	- 87,000

In order to arrive at the replacement value of each contract, the amounts would be discounted to achieve net present value (assuming a discount rate of 6%). The net positive and negative replacement values are netted to a single close-out amount due to ABC from XYZ.

Contract 1	+ 106,993
Contract 2	+ 85,202
Contract 3	- 119,658
Contract 4	- 87,000
	- 14,463

ABC Bank therefore has only USD 14,463 (less discount) in credit risk to XYZ bank at the time of default. Without the benefit of close-out netting, ABC would have USD 206,658 at risk. In other words, the sum of the cost of replacing those contracts would have caused a loss to ABC when XYZ defaulted.

The 'official' view

For many years various committees of the BIS - Angell, Lamfalussy, Noel and Allsopp - have pontificated on what should be done, but without any imposition from a central authority it would seem the individual cost per participant is too high in view of what is perceived as the tiniest likelihood of a settlement loss actually occurring.

Their combined conclusions are that multilateral netting would be an ideal way to achieve this. However, only after 5 years and $300 million has been spent on perfecting a system - now implemented in early September 2002 - where participants (currently 67 financial groups) underwrite the exchange that will handle this complex payment system which will result in one payment, per currency, per day. Currencies to be handled will be USD, CAD, EUR, AUD, JPY, GBP and CHF.

The benefits can be anticipated based on the only currently operational netting system - the bilateral FXNet - which already boasts a reduction in daily payments of 51% and a reduction in payments of 84%. Given the concentration of today's $1,230 billion per day within a maximum of 20/30 banks a likely reduction level via a multilateral system of daily payments could be as much as 90+%. Furthermore the Committee on Payment and Settlement Systems has commented that, in gross terms, the risk could be a much higher figure as:

a) each FX trade has 2 sides to settle, and;

b) the maximum settlement risk being run by an institution could be up to the value of 3 days settlements given the time taken to ensure 'finality of payment' across different time zones. Hence their reason for favouring the RTGS arrangements under the CLS Bank Ltd (see page 34 for initial data).

Conceptually anyway - bilateral or multilateral - the advantages of netting agreements can be summarised as:

1. It documents and establishes events of default - with protection for both sides.
2. Where netting is enforceable in bankruptcy, banks have the added benefit of reduced mark-to-market risk (replacement risk).
3. Reduced replacement risk can turn into lower capital requirements.
4. Netting of transactions and payments can reduce operating expense.

When it comes to mitigating market risk, banks themselves have initiated new and better ways of controlling risk:

Modern risk management methodologies

Value at Risk

It is said that when Dennis Weatherstone was Chairman of JP Morgan he demanded a daily report that summarised the company's exposure to moves in the markets and provided a decent estimate of potential losses over the next 24 hours. The result became the famous '4.15 report' delivered at that time to his office. This type of reporting, which tries to identify the potential losses based on trading positions, has become a regulatory requirement brought about by the fear of collapse through irresponsible trading.

The purpose of value at risk (VaR) is to give an estimate of losses over a short period under 'normal' market conditions. It will not tell you what might happen during a market crash. For that, stress testing and scenario analysis are necessary. Also it does not inform you of traders entering false positions (Barings being a prime example) so there must be sound operational and technical controls that help stop misuse of limits and unauthorised trading.

Once all the data has been centralised (from various trading books, other offices, etc), the overall risk has to be calculated by aggregating the risks from individual contracts across the whole portfolio. This is done by working out the effects of moves in individual risk factors (e.g. stock index, a specific point on the yield curve or swap curve, or an FX or commodity price) across the portfolio. The portfolio itself will involve large numbers of currencies and asset classes. VaR is worked out from the relationships between the individual risk factors and the effect on the portfolio of moves in each risk factor. The potential move in each risk factor has to be inferred from past price movements. For regulatory purposes the historical price movement for assessment must reflect at least one year's data, or reflect daily market movements over the previous year. This is a huge amount of data to manage for some of the smaller institutions, however JP Morgan has been distributing its data for VaR calculations free of charge.

The basis upon which VaR is calculated has been compared and contrasted and put under the microscope. A more precise definition has emerged: 'VaR is the maximum loss that will be incurred on the portfolio with a given level of confidence over a specified holding period, based on the distribution of price changes over a given historical observation period'.

The BIS rules, known as the Basel Capital Accord, specify:

- A 99% confidence interval (i.e. actual losses on the portfolio should exceed the VaR estimate not more than once every 100 days).
- A holding period of 10 days (assumes the portfolio remains unchanged for 10 days).
- A historical observation period of at least one year.

The main assumption underpinning VaR is that future price changes will be similar to past price changes upon which the risks are measured. Critics have said this is akin to driving a car by looking in the rear view mirror. It is, however, viewed as a useful tool for day-to-day risk management if it is understood that it reflects normal market conditions.

The three popular methods of calculating VaR are:

- The covariance method
- Historic volatility
- Monte Carlo simulation method

The covariance method (or correlation method)

The covariance method assumes the returns on risk factors are normally distributed, the correlations between risk factors are constant and the delta (or price sensitivity to changes in a risk factor) of each portfolio constituent is constant.

To calculate VaR the volatility of each risk factor is extracted from the historical observation period. The potential effect of each component of the portfolio on the overall portfolio is worked out from the component's delta, and that is the risk factor's volatility. These effects are then aggregated across the whole portfolio using the correlations between the risk factors to give the overall volatility of the portfolio value. The desired confidence interval for VaR can then be determined.

Historic method

Simple historic volatility is simple, however the effects of a large one-off market move can significantly distort volatilities over the forecasting period. For example, if using a 30-day historic volatility, any market shock will stay in these figures for 30 days. If past observations can be weighted unequally then more weight can be given to recent observations so that large jumps in volatility are not caused by events that happened a long time ago. However, this method still relies on the assumption that future volatilities are based on historic price movements.

It does avoid the pitfalls of the correlation (or covariance methods), i.e. normally distributed returns, constant correlations and constant deltas. These are not then needed to calculate VaR by historical simulation. Historical volatility does capture the non-normal distribution of risk factor returns. Consequently, allowance is made for one-off market events. It is, however, because of the weighting and the re-valuing of the portfolio at different levels, more computationally intensive than the covariance method.

Monte Carlo simulation method

This is the most computer intensive method of the three VaR methodologies, and also the most flexible. The risk manager will use historical distributions for risk factor returns. A large number of randomly-generated different simulations (say 10,000) are then run forward in time by using volatility and correlation estimates chosen by the risk manager. When all the simulations are done the VaR can be found by listing all the outcomes in order of profit and loss and cutting off at the required confidence level. The cutting off point represents the VaR.

Stress testing

Whichever method is used, stress testing - that is applying the equivalent of a major market movement like Black Wednesday to the VaR methodology - will ensure that the overall market risk is within the limits of the capital requirements, and can be absorbed by the financial institution.

Back testing

It is also necessary to look at past VaR reports and redefine them against what actually happened in the markets. This will ensure that the methodology employed by an institution is at least accurate to within acceptable bounds.

Sine qua non conditions for successful risk management

The mechanical actions required from the back office to assist in risk management have been detailed in the first sections of this book. In the following pages, we look at the additional factors in this area which can increase/decrease the risks.

Investigation

Back office support check confirmations

The timely despatch of the host bank's confirmations and the checking of incoming broker and counterparties' confirmations can be a critical process in the settlements environment. This is especially true where formal SSI agreements do not exist between the banks (page 47-8 of the Model Code). It is at this stage that errors not identified at the initial capture can be spotted and corrected before the value date or maturity date of the trade. (see also Case Study 6, page 177)

Undetected errors can lead to monetary losses to one or both parties to the trade and it is therefore important that confirmations received are checked for accuracy as quickly as possible. It is essential to accurately check confirmations, and to provide the technology and level of staffing to adequately complete this task, if errors and subsequent penalty claims are to be kept to a minimum.

Prompt action in identifying and correcting errors can considerably reduce or even totally avoid monetary losses being incurred by one or both parties to the trade. Internal rules should be in place that stipulate the maximum number of days that can elapse before a missing confirmation is followed up; under what circumstances matters should be referred to management, etc. Failure to adhere to these instructions could be momentous since failure to send confirmations has been the first indication that a bank is in trouble - especially when the trade would now be in a significant loss situation.

Automated Matching Systems

These systems effectively short-cut the delivery of paper-based confirmations which would need separate generation and physical delivery to the counterparty, by providing automatic electronic messages from the broker to the bank as the details are entered at the broker's office.

The specific benefits of automated matching systems are:

- Reduced risk of financial loss
- Increased security
- Improved processing efficiency
- Time saved on investigations

The specific benefits of TRAM are:

- Reduced settlement errors and related costs
- Increased productivity
- Faster matching
- Greater staff motivation
- Up-to-the-moment management information

Recording trading transactions accurately

The middle/back office

The increase in product types and the resulting surge in volumes has placed great strain on the back office. Technology development has absorbed pure volumes in relation to the increases in staffing levels, but risk is a key driver in the demand for processing systems development. Additionally, there are several factors affecting processing systems:

- Increasing volumes
- Complex instruments
- Need to reduce risk
- Need to reduce cost

These result in the simple fact that: Time = Risk = Cost. Risk varies according to currency and maturity (see Fig 8.2).

Fig 8.2 - Risk profile

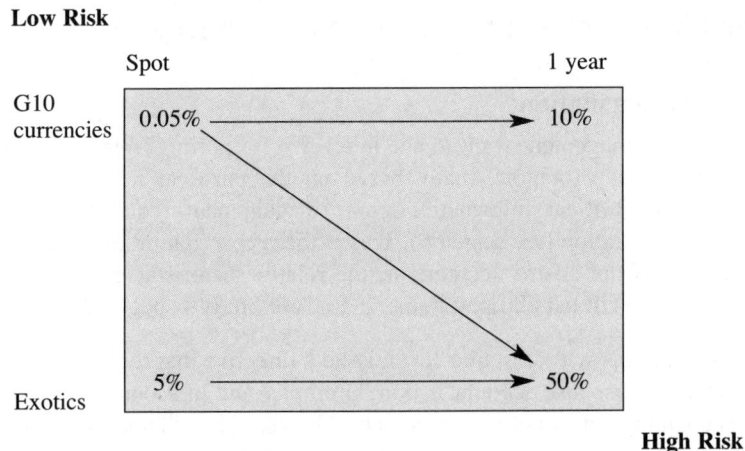

Low Risk

	Spot	1 year
G10 currencies	0.05% ⟶	10%
Exotics	5% ⟶	50%

High Risk

The solution that banks, technology vendors/developers, and Reuters and SWIFT are all focusing on is straight-through processing. As already mentioned in Chapter 2, straight through-processing is the processing of trade data with the minimum of manual intervention, the complete removal of paper from the trading process. These are tickets, confirmation faxes/telexes or payment instructions. For this to become reality there are six principles to follow:

- Capture data at its source
- Eliminate re-keying
- Encourage vendor choice
- Use modular components
- Use open systems
- Follow industry standards

Those of us who have been operation managers over the years have our concerns. What is clear is that, without very stringent controls on the trader's desk that validates his authority to trade in the product with the counterparty and within his position limits, there could be a situation where a 'Nick Leeson' result could re-occur.

Theoretically, automation will reduce this risk, but it is likely to be implemented initially with the traditional and standard market products like FX spot. The more complex products will follow, but then that is, and always has been, the way. You cannot have a system without the product, and 'rocket scientist' traders continue to create new types of products.

Providing timely information to management

Nostro reconciliation

What does management want to see in terms of reporting? Whilst there are many types of report, many based on the personal needs of the manager, the critical information/report management requires is the nostro reconciliation (see page 66). This is the reconciliation of payment in and out of the nostro accounts to the relative bank statements. The reconciliation will list all open items. (See Case Study 1, page 175)

Most institutions will, at senior level, issue a directive that reconciliation of a nostro's suspense account is done promptly and in accordance with the accounting and operation manuals. Nostro reconciliation must be done daily, and open items acted upon immediately. It is far easier to resolve investigations if acted upon immediately. The longer an item is left unresolved, the harder it becomes to clear, and the penalty claim (risk) will be significantly higher.

Nostro reconciliation should be done by a person who is not involved in:

- Originating transactions
- Responding to transactions
- Authorising transactions

The report should also contain the following:

- The difference or outstanding amount
- The product or instrument
- The trader and operational department
- The cause of the difference or outstanding amount

Any posting of penalty/loss should be accompanied by an error report, with a comment on what steps have been taken to rectify the causes. Most losses will be caused by a combination of:

- Computer/telecom fault
- Procedural deficiency
- Control failure
- Unclear instructions
- Human error
- Other

Reporting should be to the head of operations and the head of trading, and possibly the general manager. The auditing department needs to be involved in the investigation. The cash management desk of a trading, room should also be advised of any non receipts before the report is issued, as short cash positions may need to be covered promptly (market risk). Management will need to be aware of volumes of transactions and set performance targets (benchmarking) for the various steps in the transaction process. Improvements can be measured by the level of nostro outstandings in relation to the volume.

Audit support: internal and external staff

Traders and back office support groups have always been suspicious of the role of internal auditors. However an independent review of the transaction process is essential to controlling risk, from inception to settlement of a transaction. Audit has a separate reporting line, usually directly to general management and so provides that independence.

Copies of all significant reports should also be sent to audit. Here, consolidation of market and counterparty risk will take place, and reconciliation to the general ledger of the bank undertaken. Audit reports are a regular feature of operations and trading life, with reporting copied to general management or board level.

External auditors provide a further check on the bank's processes, and provide important verification of the institution's annual accounts.

One increasing area of audit concern is the control of 24-hour trading. As the euro becomes established, this area could become of yet higher focus. Although it will be management that approves/forbids such trading and sets the parameters, there will, of necessity, be a role for back office to provide separate and timely reports of all the deals contracted outside of their own centre's trading hours, and confirmation that all controls have been properly monitored, input actioned at the appropriate time, and the positions correctly adjusted before reports are sent to management. It may well also entail the maintenance and advice to other counterparties of the bank's policy, and the names of the staff authorised to carry out such activities.

Daily mark to market

When a trader takes a position in a currency or bond or option, he will have paid a price for that instrument/currency. That position is then subject to changes in price through the normal supply and demand pressures created throughout the trading day. At the end of each trading day, the close of business price is compared to the purchase price of the instrument. In this way unrealised profit or loss can be determined for the trading book.

External valuation

During the course of their annual review will review external auditors the basis upon which market risk is calculated. All annual reports must include a section on off balance sheet risk. It usually specifies the nominal value (NPV) of the forward and derivative positions and the replacement value.

Regulators - originally the SFA and the Bank of England (now both replaced by the FSA) - also kept an eye on the exposures generated by trading activities. Each financial institution will have its own regulatory body to which it must report, on a regular basis, the trading exposure. The regulatory bodies may have their own methodology on how to calculate and report market risk but the BIS capital accord is designed to generate a consistent method that is accepted and implemented internationally.

Limits

We have talked about how we determine the VaR for different currencies, settlement risks and replacement risk for counterparties and how we report these exposures to management. We need now to talk about internal limits, how they are set and how we use them in excess reporting. It is also important that each institution puts in place an effective disciplinary procedure for traders who exceed either counterparty or market limits. This should include, in the most blatant cases, dismissal.

The BIS recommendations adopted by banks by the end of 1997 (for the first time) include market risk for capital purposes. It can be argued therefore that market risk in addition to credit risk is now a cost to the bank. Therefore the setting and use of limits must be managed prudently.

Country limits

This category includes the following types of risk:

- Counterparty replacement risk relative to the country of incorporation for all traded instruments including derivatives.
- Currency risk - e.g. the exposure in VaR for the country of the relative currency.
- The relative government bonds (issuer risk).
- Eurobonds issued by non-government institutions (issuer risk). (Yankee Bonds issued in the US domestic market by a foreign borrower. The issuer risk is with the country of the issuer).
- Settlement risk (overnight).

Obviously, the main western economies (G10) are given an open limit with no constraints on total exposure at all. However careful monitoring of exposures to emerging markets or the weaker economies (e.g. some African countries) is necessary and limits need to be realistic.

From time to time approved excesses occur for good business reasons. For example, if a trader sees an arbitrage opportunity between the Swedish government bond price and the gilt, he may wish to buy as much Swedish paper as possible, having firstly been given prior approval from the banker responsible for Sweden. Country limits include all counterparty risk and, under the BIS Capital Accord, market risk originating from the respective country.

Currency limits

Most banks in the City of London trade in the main G10 currencies. Even though these countries have stable economies, it is necessary to establish limits that are indicative of the amounts or exposure measured in terms of VaR a bank is prepared to risk for, say, holding periods of overnight, 10 days, a month, etc.

The limits are set by currency or desk. The FX spot desk, for example, will have overall limits for USD, CHF, EUR, etc. The fixed income traders will have limits based on the trading book - i.e. euro sterling, US government bonds, etc., - still based on currencies of the bonds rather that the issuer.

Systems need to be developed that can apply the VaR for each currency against the limit of the desk and on to the overall limit of the currency across all products on the trading floor. Real time systems, which remain rare (only used by large investment houses or clearers) must report excessions allowing accurate decisions to be made based on client orders or large currency movements that are traded on and off the relative desks or trading books.

Duration of settlement exposure

Because we are measuring the total amount to be settled on one day with a single counterparty, technically the line begins each day at zero and, assuming everything settles, finishes the day on zero. However confirmation of settlement from, say, the US will not be received until the next morning - yet another reason for prompt nostro reconciliation. This can therefore be redefined as overnight settlement exposure.

Another type of settlement exposure is called intraday settlement exposure - e.g. the payments are made in the morning and, because of the processing delay, receipts are received in the afternoon. At around midday the intraday exposure can typically be at minus 3 billion dollars for a bank. Each bank has this same type of exposure although not quite on the same scale. Payments are made in the morning and receipts are received in the afternoon.

Stop loss/profit orders

The daily mark-to-market report will give a good indication of any specific position that is causing concern through an unrealised loss. A limit that sets the amount an institution is prepared to lose if markets move against it must be established. Some traders stick to a loss-making position because they believe it will eventually make money. However, because the trading book is for short-term investments and management may not share the same view as the trader, procedures to close out the position when a certain limit is reached must be in place.

Another aspect is when trading institutions receive requests from customers, branches and correspondents to buy or sell a fixed amount of currency if the exchange rate for that currency reaches a specified level. This type of request, which includes stop-loss and limit orders, is growing, mainly because of the increasing sophistication of risk management techniques, supported by technology development. Management therefore needs to ensure that there is a clear understanding between its institution and its counterparties regarding the basis on which these orders will be undertaken. In accepting such orders, the institution can only agree to make every reasonable effort to execute the order quickly at the established price. Disputes can occur, particularly at times of peak volume and extreme volatility, and consequent investigations may be hard to prove one way or another.

CHAPTER 9

▌▌▌

THE REGULATORY ENVIRONMENT

Starting with the 'think-tanks' at the BIS, there have been many exercises at establishing 'best practice'. The first attempt followed quite large bank losses/failures and resulted in the '8%' rule relating to capital adequacy in respect of **credit risk**.

Bank for International Settlements (BIS)

The BIS is the central bank's central bank which in 1987 brought out new capital adequacy requirements framed around a basic 8% rule. This led to the Basel Agreement of 1987, for implementation by 1993 latest. In this, the minimum targets set were:

- Capital: risk-assets of 8%
- Core capital: total capital base of 50%
- Core capital: total assets of 4%

Amendment to the Capital Accord

In April 1995 the Basel Committee on Banking Supervision issued a paper for applying capital charges to market risks incurred by banks. These risks can be defined as the risk of losses in on and off-balance sheet positions arising from movements in market prices. The instruments covered by the proposed framework are the trading book of debt and equity and related off balance sheet contracts, and foreign exchange and commodity risks. These led to the BIS recommendations (1996) which were accepted and were implemented by the G10 authorities at the end of 1997.

The risk measurement framework

As from the end of 1997, banks were required to measure and apply capital charges in respect of their **market risks** in addition to their credit risks. Market risk is defined as the risk of losses in on and off balance sheet positions arising from movements in market prices. The precise risks subject to this agreement are:

- Risks pertaining to interest rate related instruments and equities in the trading book
- Foreign exchange risk and commodities risk throughout the bank

Scope and coverage of the capital charges

The capital charges for interest rate related instruments and equities will apply to the current market value of items in bank's trading books. The trading book includes proprietary positions held for short term resale and where profits/losses are expected from movements in the price. Positions from matched principal brokering and market making, or positions taken in order to hedge other elements of the trading book are also included in the capital charge.

The banking book may be hedged or include instruments that may be used as part of the trading book. The banking book which includes proprietary positions that are for long-term investment and their respective hedges are not to be included in the market risk capital charge. In practice these investments will fall under the credit risk capital charge. Most reputable institutions have a clear division between the market traders and those employees responsible for long-term investment. The committee will monitor the way in which banks allocate financial instruments between the trading and banking books. The capital charges for foreign exchange risk and for commodities risk will apply to the bank's total currency and commodity positions.

The capital requirements for market risk are to apply on a world-wide consolidated basis. Where appropriate national authorities may permit banking and financial entities in a group which is running a global consolidated book and whose capital is being assessed on a global basis, to report long and short options in the same instrument on a net basis no matter where they are booked. However, in certain circumstances supervisory authorities may demand that the individual positions be taken into the system without any offsetting or netting against the remainder of the group.

General market risk

The capital requirement for general market risk is designed to capture the risk of loss arising from changes in interest rates. A choice between two methods, maturity and duration, is allowed. In each method the capital charge is the sum of four components:

- The net short or long position in the trading book
- A small proportion of the matched positions in each time band (the vertical disallowance)
- A larger proportion of matched positions across different time bands (the horizontal disallowance)
- A net charge for positions in options

Separate maturity ladders should be used for each currency and capital charges calculated for each currency separately and summed with no offsetting between positions of the opposite sign.

The maturity method

In the maturity method, long or short positions in debt securities and other sources of interest rate exposure, including derivatives, are slotted into a maturity ladder as shown in Table 9.1. Fixed rate instruments should be allocated according to the residual term to maturity and floating rate instruments according to the residual term to the next repricing date. Opposite positions of the same amount and maturity can be omitted.

The first step is to weight the positions in each time band by the factor designed to reflect the price sensitivity of those positions to assumed changes in interest rates. The second step is to offset the weighted longs and shorts in each time band, resulting in a single short or long position for each band. A 10% capital charge will be levied on the smaller of the offsetting positions to reflect basis and gap risk, as the positions include different instruments and maturities, e.g.

The weighted long position is $100m.
The weighted short position is $90m.

The so-called *vertical disallowance* for that time band is 10% of $90m, or $9 million.

Table 9.1 - Time bands and weights

Coupon 3% or more	Coupon less than 3%	Risk weight	Assumed changes in yield
1 mth or less	1 mth or less	0.00%	1.00
1 to 3 mths	1 to 3 mths	0.20%	1.00
3 to 6 mths	3 to 6 mths	0.40%	1.00
6 to 12 mths	6 to 12 mths	0.70%	1.00
1 to 2 yrs	1.0 to 1.9 yrs	1.25%	0.90
2 to 3 yrs	1.9 to 2.8 yrs	1.75%	0.80
3 to 4 yrs	2.8 to 3.6 yrs	2.25%	0.75
4 to 5 yrs	3.6 to 4.3 yrs	2.75%	0.75
5 to 7 yrs	4.3 to 5.7 yrs	3.25%	0.70
7 to 10 yrs	5.7 to 7.3 yrs	3.75%	0.65
10 to 15 yrs	7.3 to 9.3 yrs	4.50%	0.60
15 to 20 yrs	9.3 to 10.6 yrs	5.25%	0.60
Over 20 yrs	10.6 to 12 yrs	6.00%	0.60
	12 to 20 yrs	8.00%	0.60
	Over 20 yrs	12.50%	0.60

This calculation produces two sets of weighted positions. The net long or short position in each time band ($10m in the above example), and the vertical disallowance.

In addition, banks are allowed to conduct two rounds of horizontal offsetting. Firstly between the net position in the three different time bands (0 to 1 year, 1 to 4 years and 4 years and over) and subsequently between the net positions in the three different time bands. The offsetting is subject to a scale of disallowances expressed as a fraction of the matched positions (see Table 9.2). The weighted long and short positions in each of the three zones may be offset, subject to the matched portion attracting a disallowance factor that is part of the capital charge. The residual net position in each zone may be carried over and offset against opposite positions in other zones to a second set of disallowance factors.

Table 9.2 - Horizontal disallowances

Zone	Time band	Within the zone	Between adjacent zones	Between zones 1 and 2
1	0 to 1 mth 1 to 3 mths 3 to 6 mths 6 to 12 mths	40%	40%	100%
2	1 to 2 yrs 2 to 3 yrs 3 to 4 yrs	30%		
3	4 to 5 yrs 5 to 7 yrs 7 to 10 yrs 10 to 15 yrs 15 to 20 yrs Over 20 yrs	30%	40%	

The duration method

This is a more accurate method of measuring general risk in which banks measure all their general market risk by calculating the price sensitivity of each position separately. This requires supervisory consent and will be subject to supervisory monitoring of the systems used to calculate the sensitivity.

The mechanics of this method are as follows:

- First, calculate the price sensitivity of each instrument in terms of an interest rate change in interest rates of between 0.6 and 1.0 percentage points depending on the maturity of the instrument.

- Slot the resulting sensitivity measure into the duration-based ladder (see Table 9.3).

- Subject long and short positions in each time band to a 5% vertical disallowance designed to capture basis risk.

- Carry forward the net positions in each time band for horizontal offsetting subject to the disallowances set out in the horizontal disallowance (see Table 9.2).

Interest rate derivatives

Interest rate derivatives are FRAs, bond futures, interest rate and cross currency swaps and forward FX positions. They should also be converted into positions in the relevant underlying, and become subject to the charges as described in Table 9.4. The amounts reported should be the market value of the principal amount of the underlying or of the notional underlying.

Futures and FRAs are treated as a combination of a long and a short position in a notional government security. The maturity of a future or FRA will be the period until delivery or exercise of the contract plus, where applicable, the life of the underlying instrument. For example, a long position in a June three-month interest rate future taken in April is to be reported as a long position in a government security with a maturity of five months and a short position in a government security with a maturity of two months.

Table 9.3 - Duration method: time bands and assumed changes in yield

Zone	Time band	Assumed change in yield
Zone 1	1 mth or less	1.00
	1 to 3 mths	1.00
	3 to 6 mths	1.00
	6 to 12 mths	1.00
Zone 2	1.0 to 1.9 yrs	0.90
	1.9 to 2.8 yrs	0.80
	2.8 to 3.6 yrs	0.75
Zone 3	3.6 to 4.5 yrs	0.75
	4.3 to 5.7 yrs	0.70
	5.7 to 7.3 yrs	0.65
	7.3 to 9.3 yrs	0.60
	9.3 to 10.6 yrs	0.60
	10.6 to 12 yrs	0.60
	12 to 20 yrs	0/60
	Over 20 yrs	0.60

Swaps are treated as two notional positions in government securities with relevant maturities. If a bank is receiving floating and paying fixed, this is seen as a long position in an instrument with a maturity at the next repricing date and a short position in a fixed rate instrument with the maturity of the residual life of the swap.

Calculation of capital charges under the standardised methodology

Allowable offsets

Excluded from the calculation are long and short positions in identical instruments with exactly the same issue, coupon, currency and maturity. Also excluded is a matched position in a future or forward and its corresponding underlying. There is no offsetting in positions in different currencies: the separate legs of a cross currency swap or FX forwards are to be treated as notional positions in the relevant instruments and included in the calculation for each currency.

Additionally, offsets in certain conditions are allowed in the following cases:

- The underlying must be of the same nominal value and denominated in the same currency.

- For futures: the products must be identical and mature within seven days of each other.

- For swaps and FRAs: the reference rate (for floating rate positions) must be identical and the coupon closely matched (within 15 basis points).

- For swaps, FRAs and forwards: the next interest fixing day, or for fixed coupon positions or forwards, the residual maturity must correspond within the following limits:

    - Less than one month, hence same day.
    - Between one month and one year, hence within seven days.
    - Over one year, hence within 30 days.

Flexibility in approach is allowed if approved by the supervisory authority (see Table 9.4) and regularly monitored. For example, institutions with large swap books may wish to convert the payments into present value and a single net figure entered into the appropriate time band using procedures that apply to zero or low coupon bonds.

Table 9.4 - Summary of treatment of interest rate derivatives

Instrument	Specific risk charge	General market risk charge
Exchange traded future		
Government debt security	No	Yes, as two positions
Corporate debt security	Yes	Yes, as two positions
Index on interest rates	No	Yes, as two positions
OTC forward		
Government debt security	No	Yes, as two positions
Corporate debt security	Yes	Yes, as two positions
Index on interest rates	No	Yes, as two positions
FRAs/swaps	No	Yes, as two positions
Forward foreign exchange	No	Yes, as two positions

Interest rate and currency swaps, FRAs, forward FX contracts and interest rate futures on an interest rate index (e.g. LIBOR) will not be subject to a specific risk charge (e.g. credit).

Table 9.5 - BIS Triennial Survey of Market Turnover

• FX Turnover 2001 1.2 billion per day down 19% on 1998 figure of 1.49 billion per day.

• Derivative Turnover 2001 575 billion per day up 53% on 1998 figure of 375 billion per day - mostly interest rate derivatives showing the large increases while currency options fell.

Average FX Daily Turnover			
Country	April 2001 ($bn)	2001 %age Share	April 1998 ($bn)
UK	504	31.1	637
US	254	15.7	350
Japan	147	9.1	149
Singapore	101	6.2	139
Germany	88	5.4	94
Switzerland	71	4.4	82
Hong Kong	67	4.1	79
Australia	52	3.2	47
France	48	3.0	72

OTC Derivative Average Daily Turnover			
Country	April 2001 ($bn)	2001 %age Share	April 1998 ($bn)
UK	275	36.0	171
US	135	17.7	91
Germany	97	12.7	34
France	67	8.8	46
Japan	22	2.9	42
Switzerland	15	2.0	15
Australia	12	1.6	5
Singapore	6	0.8	11
Hong Kong	4	0.5	4

Each category of asset was given a weighting to arrive at a 'risk-assets' figure, for example:

- Domestic government: Nil
- Cash: Nil
- Claims on other OECD banks: 20%
- Mortgage loans to owner-occupiers: 50%
- Other claims on the non-bank private sector: 100%
- Claims on non-OECD banks: 100%
- Aggregate net short open FX positions: 100%

Similarly, each type of off-balance sheet instrument was given a weighting. This was set at 8% of the default risk - effectively 8% of any contract that is in profit - when marked-to-market. However, all off-balance sheet (OBS) instruments carry far lower weightings, and thus permit considerable leverage and hedging potential.

Since the initial capital adequacy requirements were introduced, some refinements have been put in place via the Capital Adequacy Directive (CAD) of 1996 which extended minimum capital requirements upon all credit institutions and investment firms in respect of market risk and other risks associated with the trading book, i.e. beyond counterparty risk and instrument risk. CAD introduced the differentiation between a banking book and a trading book with a distinction between the two's risk profile.

At the same time a new tier of capital was introduced. Tier 3 equals up to two years subordinated debt and daily net trading profits, to be used principally to support the trading book. This change was made to allow the use of more flexible forms of capital to support risks arising from the trading book. To do this, the whole risk on the trading book as a whole will be assessed value at risk (VaR) instead of assessing each component part. This new approach would normally reduce the total value of risk-weighted assets and thus the capital required. As a result, the Basel Committee confirmed in 1996 the new approach to regulation in that:

- Market risk will be formally considered for supervisory purposes.

- A concession is now made to the commercial banks to use their own VaR models although they will be required to meet specific qualitative and quantitative criteria.

Division of risks

Each financial institution must now divide its balance sheet into a banking book and a trading book. Effectively this means that the 'normal' business of a bank is included in the 'banking' book with all the short-term speculative business in the 'trading' book. Thus the trading book contains:

- Transferable securities and units in collective investments
- Money market instruments, not deposits and loans
- Financial futures contracts, including cash settled instruments
- FRAs
- Interest rate, currency and equity swaps
- Options on all of the above, especially on currency and interest rates

The banking book still needs capital, but as specified under the original Basel 8% rules. The trading book is covering more than just counterparty risk and has to have its own rules, and this has led to the creation of an additional tier of capital - Tier 3. Capital is thus now considered under:

Tier 1 - Core capital

> Permanent shareholders equity
> Allotted, called and fully paid-up preferred stock
> Disclosed reserves
> Interim declared profits (audited)
> Minority interests

Tier 2 - Supplementary capital

> Reserves resulting from revalued fixed assets
> General provisions
> Hybrid capital - perpetual cumulative preferred shares and perpetual subordinated debt
> Subordinated term debt

Tier 3 - Trading book ancillary capital

> Short-term subordinated debt, minimum two years original
> Daily net trading book profits

- The total of Tier 2 cannot exceed 50% of Tier 1.

- Tier 2 capital used to meet banking book cannot exceed 100% of Tier 1 used for the same purpose.

- Tier 2 and Tier 3 used to meet trading book capital must not in total exceed 200% of the Tier 1 capital used for same purpose.

- The total of Tier 2 and Tier 3 cannot normally exceed Tier 1.

The treatment of foreign currencies

Two processes are needed to calculate the capital requirement for foreign exchange risk:

- Measure the exposure in a single currency position.
- Measure the risks inherent in a bank's mix of long and short positions.

Measuring the exposure in a single currency

The bank's net open position in each currency should be calculated by summing:

- The net spot position (assets less liabilities, including accrued interest in the currency in question);

- The net forward position (including currency futures and principals on currency swaps not included in the spot position);

- Guarantees that are certain to be called and are likely to be irrecoverable;

- Net future income/expenses not yet accrued but already fully hedged;

- Any other item representing a profit or loss in foreign currencies;

- The net delta-based equivalent of the total book of foreign currency options

Composite currencies such as the ECU could, until January 1999, be either reported as a separate currency or split into their component parts. Interest accrued should be included as a position. Accrued expenses should also be included.

Forward currency positions will be valued at the current spot rate.

However, if banks value their positions using NPV then it is expected that this is the value to be included for the capital charge. No capital charge need apply to positions related to items that are deducted from a bank's capital base such as investments in a non-consolidated subsidiary.

Measuring the FX risk in a portfolio of foreign currency positions

Banks may either use a method described in Table 9.6 which treats all currencies equally, or use an internal model that calculates the degree of risk dependant on the composition of the bank's portfolio.

Table 9.6 - Calculation of capital requirement from FX position

Yen	DEM	GBP	FFR	US$	Gold
+50	+100	+150	-20	-180	-35
	+300		-200		-35

The NPV of each currency is converted at spot rates into the reporting currency. The overall net position is measured by aggregating the sum of the net short positions or the sum of the net long positions, whichever is the greater, plus the net position (short or long) in gold (if traded). The capital charge would be 8% of the higher of either the net long currency positions or the net short currency positions (i.e. 300) and the net position in gold (35) = 335 x 8% = 26.8.

Asset liability risk management methodology

The simplest techniques for measuring a bank's interest rate exposure is to allocate interest sensitive assets and liabilities and related off-balance sheet positions into a certain number of predefined time bands according to their maturity. If fixed rate, until maturity; if floating rate, until their next re-pricing. Assets or liabilities lacking a definitive maturity, for example, demand deposit accounts (DDA) or savings accounts, are assigned to re-pricing bands based on the judgement and past experience of the bank.

Gap analysis

Using the time band allocation, assets and liabilities can be netted, in accordance with their maturity bands, to produce a repricing 'gap' for that time band. This gap can be multiplied by an assumed change in interest rates to yield an approximation of the change in net interest income that would result from such an interest rate movement. The size of the interest rate movement used can be based on a variety of factors, including historical data, estimates of future rate movements and internal judgements.

A negative gap occurs when liabilities exceed assets (including off-balance sheet positions). If an increase in interest rates occurs then there would be a decline in net interest income. Conversely, a positive or asset -sensitive gap implies the bank's net interest income could decline if there was a decrease in the level of interest rates.

This approach, however, does have a number of shortcomings that results in the approximation of the true risk. Gap analysis does not take into account the variation in characteristics in the different instruments within each time band. They are assumed to mature or reprice simultaneously. Gap analysis also ignores the differences in spreads between interest rates that could arise through basis risk. Finally, it does not take into account any changes in the timing of payments that may occur as a result of changes in the interest rate environment - i.e. exercising American OTC interest rate options or time options.

Duration analysis

This relates to yield curve risk. Simply put, duration analysis measures changes in economic value resulting from a percentage change of interest rates under the assumption that changes in value are proportional to changes in the level of interest rates, and the timing of payments is fixed. By applying sensitivity weights to each time band, the effects of changing interest rates can be evaluated. Here we look at the estimated duration of the asset/liability rather than the precise maturity/repricing date.

Used in combination with the maturity/repricing schedule, the duration-weighted gaps are aggregated across time bands to produce an estimate of the change in the economic value of the bank. Banks can, by using a precise duration of each asset/liability, determine a net position for each asset/liability more accurately. An alternative approach would be to design risk weights on the basis of actual percentage changes of hypothetical instruments for each time band, as opposed to the interest rate gap profile. This approach, 'effective duration', would better capture the non-linearity of price movements arising from significant changes in market interest rates.

Simulation approaches

Many of the larger, more sophisticated banks employ more complex interest rate measurement systems. The simulation techniques include more detailed assessments of the potential effects in interest rate earnings. This involves a more detailed breakdown of the various categories on and off the balance sheet. It allows for specific assumptions about the interest and principal payments, and non-interest income and expense arising from each type of position can be incorporated. Sensitivity analysis can also be developed by incorporating more varied and refined changes in the interest rate environment. This includes changes to the slope and shape of the yield curve.

A dynamic simulation looks at changes in the bank's interest rate policy and strategy. This would quantify the risks of such changes in policy. In any risk evaluation system, be it sophisticated or not, the accuracy of the underlying information is essential for an effective and accurate risk management process.

CAD II

As if that were not enough - with the implications of the 8% rule leading to strict capital requirements re credit risk, and the CAD increasing that for market risk, we now have to consider 'son of CAD' (or CAD II) re capital requirements in respect of operational risk. Although the recommendations are at an early stage, the eventual implementation is scheduled for 2004. Individual banks are already planning ahead and examining each area on which CAD II comments to see how they measure up to its views.

Essentially, CAD II is a review of the original 1988 8% rule, amended to take account of what has happened over the intervening years. For those banks which can prove that they have been more than sensible in their approach to all categories of risk there will be benefits as regards their capital requirements under the new regime.

Rationale for the New Accord: need for more flexibility and risk sensitivity

More than a decade has passed since the Basel Committee on Banking Supervision (the Committee) introduced its 1988 Capital Accord (the Accord). The business of banking, risk management practices, supervisory approaches, and financial markets have each undergone significant transformation since then.

The 1988 Accord focused on the total amount of capital required to prevent bank insolvency and potential knock-on cost to a bank's depositors. CAD II builds on that by placing more emphasis on a bank's own internal control and management, the supervisory review process and market discipline.

The 1988 Accord essentially provided only one option for measuring the appropriate capital of internationally active banks, whereas the best way to measure, manage and mitigate risks, differs from bank to bank. An Amendment was introduced in 1996 which focussed on trading risks and allowed some banks for the first time to use their own systems to measure their market risks.

The new Accord builds on that flexibility by providing varying approaches from simple to advanced for measuring both market and operational risk. Banks will be allowed to choose which one fits their level of sophistication and risk appetite/exposures. It does this by providing a spectrum of approaches from simple to advanced methodologies for the measurement of both credit risk and operational risk in determining capital levels.

Thus capital will be more in line with each individual bank's underlying risks, thereby allowing a bank to manage its business more efficiently. Although more complex it is less prescriptive - not a 'one size fits all' approach - and thus individually more appropriate, offers a flexible structure for banks to adopt approaches which best suit their degree of sophistication and risk profile. It also builds in rewards for better risk management.

Safety and soundness in today's dynamic and complex financial system can be attained only by the combination of effective bank-level management, market discipline, and supervision. The 1988 Accord focussed on the total amount of bank capital, which is vital in reducing the risk of bank insolvency and the potential cost of a bank's failure for

147

depositions. Building on this, the new framework intends to improve safety and soundness in the financial system by placing more emphasis on bank's own internal control and management (1st pillar), the supervisory review process (2nd pillar), and market discipline (3rd pillar).

Although the new framework's focus is primarily on internationally active banks, its underlying principles are intended to be suitable for application to banks of varying levels of complexity and sophistication. The committee has consulted with supervisors world-wide in developing the new framework and expects the New Accord to be adhered to by all significant banks within a certain period of time.

How will CAD II work?

The New Accord has three mutually reinforcing pillars:

The first pillar: minimum capital requirement

How capital adequacy is measured:

The first pillar maintains both the current definition of capital and the minimum requirement of 8% of capital to risk-weighted assets. To ensure that risk within a whole group is taken into consideration, the New Accord will be extended on a consolidated basis to holding companies of banking groups.

Credit risk

The methods are now more elaborate. For the measurement of credit risk, two principal options are being proposed. The first is the standardised approach, and the second the internal rating based (IRB) approach. There are two variants of the IRB approach, foundation and advanced. The use of the IRB approach will be subject to approval by the supervisor, based on the standards established by the Committee.

The standardised approach for credit risk

This is in concept the same as under current arrangements, but more risk sensitive. Banks allocate a risk-weight to each asset and OBS positions and produce a sum of risk-weighted assets. A risk weight of 100% means it is included at its full value - for corporate lending, the existing Accord provides only one risk weight category of 100% but the New Accord will provide four categories (20%, 50%, 100% and 150%) linked to external rating agency assessments.

The internal ratings based approach (IRB)

Banks will be allowed to use their own internal estimates of client' credit worthiness when assessing risk in their portfolios. Distinct and approved analytical procedures will be required - for example corporate and retail lending, whose loss characteristics are different.

The foundation method allows banks to estimate probability of default, with the supervisory authority supplying other inputs. The more advanced method will apply when it is deemed that a bank has a sufficiently developed internal allocation process, and the bank will be allowed to supply the other inputs too. Both methods will have a greater range of weightings.

Credit risk mitigation and securitisation

The new framework introduces more risk-sensitive approaches to the treatment of collateral, guarantees, credit derivatives, netting and securitisation, under both the standardised approach and the IRB approach.

Operational risk

This is the new factor to be taken into account and covers - for example, the risk of loss from computer failures, poor documentation or fraud.

There are 3 methodologies envisaged: basic indicator, standardised, and internal measurement.

* Basic indicator - uses one indicator over total activity without any variation.

* Standardised - uses different indicators for different lines of business.

* Internal - allows individual banks to utilise their internal loss data in the estimation of required capital.

The operational part of overall capital required for an institution is anticipated as being approximately 20% of total capital, and the overall capital is neither meant to rise nor fall per se, but potential gains in the best-controlled institutions,are expected to accrue.

Both Pillars 2 and 3 have implications for the training and expertise of bank supervisors.

The second pillar: supervisory review process

An external authority (like the FSA in UK) needs to ensure that the internal processes of banks which they supervise are rigorous and address each bank's particular risk profile. This requirement clearly has implications for the training and expertise of bank supervisors.

The third pillar: market discipline

The purpose of this pillar is to engender greater market discipline via enhanced disclosure. If a bank is 'transparent' about the methods it is using, the method of making its calculations and risk assessment, then any gaps should be more easily spotted by the supervisory authorities. Also more details will be required on how individual banks' systems of credit risk assessment, credit risk mitigation and asset securitisation are applied.

Summary

As far as the amount of overall capital is concerned, the intention is neither to raise nor to lower it. Within the overall approach, the committee would like to see a move from the standardised to the IRB method.

Practical implications

The second pillar ensures that the supervisory bodies themselves:

a) exert pressure on institutions to put the necessary control and review processes in force; and

b) supervise the internal capital assessment process and setting of targets to suit each bank's risk profile. This should lead to the establishment of sound internal processes, and greater dialogue between bank and supervisor.

The effects of the 2nd pillar should in turn lead to fulfilment of the 3rd pillar - market discipline. Strong internal processes and greater dialogue between bank and supervisor will result in enhanced disclosure and transparency.

When it comes to implementing the new requirements an institution must prove that:

Its risk management environment is conceptually sound.

It is implemented with integrity.

It has sufficient numbers of skilled staff who can use sophisticated models not just in the trading area but in risk control, audit and where necessary - in back office.

The models being used are FSA approved, have a proven track record and back-testing record.

There are regular stress tests conducted on the models.

The infrastructure and support areas have established and robust processes to cope with a multi-product, multi-risk and multi-currency business.

The areas covered will have to include:

1. Current control procedures - what they are, how often they occur, what seniority of staff are in control re deal confirmation / error / tracking / logging / reconciliation. Proper planning for new products and/or product expansion.

2. Level of reporting - again what, when and by whom.

3. Follow-up/escalation procedures.

4. Knowledge of and understanding of back office systems - and their shortfalls.

5. Understanding of market risk principles and limit structures.

6. Management information - who gets what and when + follow-up procedures.

7. Training - in view of FSA CDP requirements a clear set of principles re training, especially of key staff, will have to be shown.

Ahead of negotiations with the authorities, an institution needs to gather together all heads of departments:

Treasury / back office / middle office / accounts / audit / IT / risk / finance etc to vet existing procedures/ staff/ systems. The aim is to seek out weak points, test existing systems and draw up check-lists/lists of procedures on which to judge performance.

All this is necessary in order to be able to cope with the FSA questionnaire that will precede visits, and interviews with staff as a part of the process for CAD II approval.

CHAPTER 10

▌▌▌

EQUITIES

This chapter, for reasons explained below, can only be an outline given the lack of uniformity in markets, systems and regulations.

Equity markets exist across the globe, and activity in stocks and shares, stock indices and options, plus options on individual stocks are very heavily traded. As stated elsewhere, there is so much interlinking between the Foreign Exchange, Money Markets and Equities, that movements out of one are reflected by moves into one of the others.

Normally the operations area of a bank that handles Treasury transactions would not also handle settlements in equities. One of the main reasons for this would be the fact that the homogeneous nature of Treasury operations the world over is not repeated in equity markets.

Variations in world equity markets

Equity markets vary in:

Settlement dates - anything from trade +1 to trade +7

Nature of stocks - some stocks are 'dematerialised' - i.e. held on an electronic register, some settle with actual scrip (share certificates)

Nature of trading/matching - some exchanges offer electronic matching on a FIFO basis; some on an 'all or nothing' basis, some on part fills.

Securities traded - only individual shares of that country; international companies registered on another exchange via Depository Receipts; Stock Indices such as FTSE Index, S&P Index or Nikkei 225 Index; options on these same indices; options on individual shares

Thus, life is difficult for the settlements area in an active equity-trading institution due to the matrix of possible settlement requirements. One good thing is that the majority of active exchanges offer an electronic processing system - if you can afford to be part of it.

Securities settlements

The 1987 crash prompted regulators to review securities settlement procedures with a view to reducing or eliminating principal risk. This is similar to cross-currency risk in foreign exchange settlements - i.e. the risk that a seller of a security could deliver a security but not receive payment, or vice versa.

The Committee for Payments and Settlement Systems (CPSS) concluded that the best way of eliminating principal risk was the creation of delivery-versus-payment (DVP) systems. The following is a summary of its report (the full documents are referred to in the summary and can be accessed via the CPSS website):

The **three** main types of DVP systems in use in G10 countries are:

1. Systems that settle transfer instructions for both securities and funds on a trade-by-trade (gross) basis, with final (unconditional) transfer of securities from the seller to the buyer (delivery) occurring at the same time as final transfer of funds from the buyer to the seller (payment).

2. Systems that settle securities transfer instructions on a gross basis with final transfer of securities from the seller to the buyer (delivery) occurring throughout the processing cycle, but settle funds transfer instructions on a net basis, with final transfer of funds from the buyer to the seller (payment) occurring at the end of the processing cycle.

3. Systems that settle transfer instructions for both securities and funds on a net basis, with final transfers of both securities and funds occurring at the end of the processing cycle.

The implications of DVP systems and their alternatives are found in *'Delivery versus Payment in Securities Settlement Systems'* (1992).

The DVP report was limited because it only examined securities settlements between two direct participants in a local system. With international securities trading on the increase, the CPSS decided to look also at the risks of settling internationally. *'Cross-Border Securities Settlements'* (1995) analyses the main channels that market participants use. These are - a local agent, a global custodian, an international central securities depository (ICSD) and using a bilateral link between central securities depositories (CSDs). The report outlines the different risks of each arrangement.

The report stresses the importance of understanding custody risks which it says will be present in any cross-border system where participants hold their securities through an intermediary, a standard practice for non-residents attempting to settle cross-border transactions.

To a greater degree than is typically the case in domestic settlements, risks in cross-border settlements are concentrated in such intermediaries, especially in the ICSDs and in local agents that settle on behalf of international securities houses. The report concludes that the complexity of relationships between the multiple intermediaries poses challenges to the supervision of domestic markets and settlement systems.

Investors in emerging markets have found clearance and settlement procedures in such markets to be wanting in terms of efficiency. In 1989, the G-30 recommended that each domestic market should establish a central securities depository (CSD) to hold securities, believing that such a move would facilitate more efficient settlement procedures.

In September 1996, the Emerging Markets Committee of the International Organisation of Securities Commission was asked to study the prerequisites of an efficient clearing and settlement system. In its report, *'Towards a Legal Framework for Clearing and Settlement in Emerging Markets'* (1997), the committee noted that the legal framework of many of these countries is still based on the concept of physical delivery which does not exist in a modern central depository system where securities are held in either immobilised or completely scriptless forms, and are transferred from one party to another via book-entries.

The report provides guidelines for the development of legal and regulatory policies to support automated clearing systems and central securities depositories.

Key Steps in Clearance and Settlement

The process of clearing and settling a securities trade includes a number of key steps, including the **matching** of the terms of the trade, the calculation of the obligations of the counterparties as a consequence of matched trades (**clearance**), the discharge of those obligations (settlement) through the final transfer of securities (**delivery**) and the final transfer of funds (**payment**).

Although a number of these steps may not directly involve the securities **settlement system**, an understanding of each of the steps is essential to an understanding of the nature and sources of risk that are faced by the operator of the settlement system or by other participants in the system.

The process begins with the execution of the trade. A variety of trade execution systems are in use in the G10 countries, ranging from the 'open outcry' systems that have traditionally been used on stock exchanges, to the networks of telecommunications links that have traditionally been used in the over-the-counter markets, to automated trade execution systems based on links between computers.

Once a trade is executed, the next step is to ensure that the counterparties to the trade (the buyer and the seller) agree on the terms of the transaction - the security involved, the price, the amount to be exchanged, the settlement date and the counterparty. This step is referred to in some markets as trade matching and in others as trade comparison or checking.

In automated trade execution systems, counterparties often agree that trades will settle as recorded at the time of execution unless both agree to a cancellation; such trades are referred to as 'locked-in' trades. In other trade execution systems matching is typically performed by an exchange, a clearing corporation or trade association, or by the settlement system.

Direct market participants may execute trades not only for their own accounts but also for the accounts of customers, including institutional investors and retail investors. In this case, the direct market participant may be required to notify its customer (or its agent) of the details of the trade and allow the customer to positively affirm the details, a process referred to as trade **confirmation** or affirmation.

As part of its overall strategy to reduce delays between the execution of a trade and its settlement, the Group of Thirty had already recommended that by 1990 trade matching should be accomplished by trade date plus one day (T+1) and that by 1992 institutional investors should be members of a trade confirmation system.

Once the obligations of the market participants have been calculated, whether on a gross basis, a bilateral net basis or a multilateral net basis, the instructions to transfer the securities and funds (money) necessary to discharge the obligations must be transmitted to the entity or entities that operate the settlement system.

These instructions may be prepared by the counterparties themselves or by an exchange or **clearing system** (which may perform trade matching and perhaps netting as well). If trades have not previously been matched, the settlement system would typically perform this function before initiating processing of the transfer instructions.

Other action may be required of participants before settlement can proceed, such as the pre-positioning of securities, funds or collateral. The time required to complete these and previous steps currently varies greatly from market to market. The Group of Thirty recommended that settlement occur no later than T+3.

Settlement of a securities trade involves the transfer of the securities from the seller to the buyer and the transfer of funds from the buyer to the seller. Historically, securities transfers involved the physical movement of **certificates**. However, in recent years securities transfers have increasingly occurred by **book-entry**.

This trend has been supported by the Group of Thirty, which recommended the establishment of, and broadest possible participation in, **central securities depositories** that provide a facility for holding securities in either a certificated or an **uncertificated (dematerialised)** form and permit the transfer of these holdings through book-entry.

A central securities depository may also offer funds accounts and permit funds transfers as a means of payment, or funds transfers may occur on the books of another institution, such as a commercial bank or central bank. In some cases (most often for government securities), the central bank operates the central securities depository, while in other cases it is operated by a private entity.

Alternative Channels for Settling Cross-Border Trades

A non-resident could settle its trades through any of as many as five different channels:

1. Through direct access to (membership of) the CSD in the country of issue;

2. Through a local agent (a local bank that is a member of the CSD in the country of issue);

3. Through a global custodian that employs a local agent as sub-custodian;

4. Through an ICSD that has established a direct or indirect (through a local agent) link to the CSD in the country of issue; or

5. Through a CSD in the non-resident's own country that has established a link (usually direct) to the CSD in the country of issue.

Risk in Cross-Border Settlements

With respect to ways of achieving DVP (or, perhaps more accurately, of linking a funds transfer system to a securities transfer system (a CSD)), the G10 countries revealed a wide variety of approaches. Although not all of these arrangements could be fitted neatly into any simple rule, three broad structural approaches were acknowledged by the BIS:

The strength of a system depends critically on the safeguards employed by the system operator to limit potential losses and liquidity pressures from such a failure. The BIS's review of systems in the G10 countries revealed that the safeguards employed varied considerably from system to system. All of the systems that were reviewed employed membership standards for participants, but the use of other risk controls was far from uniform.

The other inherent difference stems from the need for non-resident counterparties to effect money settlements in foreign currencies. A non-resident usually needs banking facilities in the country of issue of the currency used in the settlement, and it may be able to meet a substantial part of its liquidity needs in the local market. Nonetheless, a non-resident may often need to supplement its liquidity in the local currency by drawing on liquidity in its home country and converting the proceeds into the local currency through foreign exchange transactions.

More important than these inherent differences, however, is the fact that the analysis presented by the BIS is limited in certain respects, and those limitations are generally far more significant in a cross-border context than in a domestic context. By far the most important limitation is that the BIS report focused heavily on the settlement by individual CSDs of trades between their direct participants.

Even in domestic settlement systems, many buyers and sellers of securities are not direct participants in the CSD. Participation is typically restricted to banks and broker-dealers, and many banks and broker-dealers choose not to participate directly. Instead, they hold their securities and settle their trades through custodian banks (local agents). But, as discussed in the previous section, in a cross-border context the use of local agents or other intermediaries for holding securities and effecting settlements is pervasive, and the BIS's focus on direct participants is a critical limitation.

Another point that is quite important in a cross-border context, but that was not addressed in the BIS report, is the risk associated with cross-system settlements - that is, settlements effected through links between securities transfer systems.

Increases in cross-border trading and in the demand for back-to-back settlement of such trades have encouraged the development of such links. But cross-system settlements often involve significant inefficiencies that derive from the need for the transfer systems to exchange information on whether the two counterparties have the securities and funds (or access to credit) necessary to complete settlement. In particular, the settlement of back-to-back trades in which one or both settlements are cross-system settlements is often not possible, so that dealers are obliged to pre-position or borrow securities to complete such settlements.

In general, the risks associated with cross-border settlements, and how significantly they differ from those involved in direct settlement in the local CSD, depend on the trading and financing patterns of non-resident counterparties and on the specific services provided by the intermediaries that they employ to hold their securities and settle their trades.

Settlement through a local agent

A local agent typically holds securities and settles trades for non-residents through an account that it maintains at the local CSD. Usually the customers' securities are segregated from the local agent's own securities on the books of the CSD. In most cases, the customer's securities are held collectively in a single omnibus account, although some CSDs offer custodians the option of setting up sub-accounts for individual customers.

Trades of non-residents which settle through a local agent generally settle according to the same rules and procedures as any other trades settled by the CSD; thus, such non-residents are, in effect, indirect participants in the CSD. In that case, the settlement risks arising in cross-border trades settled through this channel are in many respects identical to the risks faced by direct participants in the local CSD Perhaps the most basic difference in risks is that the non-resident faces custody risk - the potential loss of the securities held in custody in the event that the local agent becomes insolvent, acts negligently or commits fraud.

Settlement through a global custodian

As in the case of settlement through a local agent, the risks associated with a non-resident counterparty's settlement through a global custodian are similar in many respects to the risks faced by a direct participant in the local CSD. The similarities reflect the fact that a global custodian settles the non-resident counterparty's trades through a local agent acting as sub-custodian.

The local agent, in turn, usually settles those trades through an account that it maintains at the local CSD, subject to the local CSD's rules and procedures. Thus, whether the settlement of a non-resident's trades through a global custodian entails principal risk depends on whether the local CSD achieves DVP.

Bearing in mind that the above is but a summary - with much more detail in the full papers cited - it is easy to envisage the potential difficulty of settling equities which have been traded in several different markets. Each exchange does offer significant assistance to potential clients, both in brochures and personal, tailor-made advice.

After all, it is only a question of ensuring cash moves one way and the stock/share the other . . . if only it were that easy!

However, it is not impossible - just as long as you realise that the rules etc. vary a lot from one stock exchange to another. Hopefully your dealers will choose to deal on just a few exchanges, where English is a common language and systems are so well-designed that the likelihood of major problems in settling is low.

SELF TESTS

III

Questions

1. The general management has announced that settlements and the FX trading desk will have to co-locate next to each other on the same floor as part of a cost-saving exercise. You are responsible for control within settlements. Outline your concerns and the measures that you would take to resolve them.

2. Describe the FX confirmation process, covering the reasons for sending confirmations, the advantages and disadvantages of the different methods of confirming and the control framework surrounding confirmations.

3. Describe briefly each of the following three topics:
   a. Netting
   b. Nostro reconciliations
   c. Collateral

4. Explain FX settlement risk and briefly outline the initiatives being taken to reduce this risk.

5. Explain real time gross settlement and briefly outline its benefits.

6. What are delivery versus payment (DVP) and payment versus payment (PVP) and their benefits?

7. Describe the advantages of SSIs when compared with deal-by-deal exchange of instructions.

8. What are the benefits of using the central money office (CMO) to deliver sterling securities?

Answer to Question 1

> *'The general management has announced that settlements and the FX trading desk will have to co-locate next to each other on the same floor as part of a cost-saving exercise. You are responsible for control within settlements. Outline your concerns and the measures that you would take to resolve them'.*

The overriding concern relates to the segregation of duties between operations personnel and sales and trading personnel. Put very simply, this means there should be a clear split between the duties of the two functions, i.e. the front office should enter into transactions, the back office should confirm and settle those transactions. Each should not undertake the other's functions. Without this basic segregation the risk of fraud arises, as has been evidenced recently at both Barings PLC and Daiwa Bank.

Whilst it is always preferable to have distinct physical separation, (e.g. different buildings, floors or offices), a lack of such segregation may be acceptable, provided that it can be demonstrated that appropriate management controls (shown below) are in place. In any case, some basic separation, e.g. screens, cupboards, etc., should be used wherever possible.

Operations personnel, who are responsible for confirmation and settlement, must maintain a reporting line independent of sales and trading, where the trade execution takes place.

Basic 'segregation' controls should be in place, for example, computer logical access controls. These ensure that front office personnel cannot access settlements systems and back office personnel cannot access deal capture systems (or relevant functionality contained therein).

Confirmations should be sent directly to, and from, back office staff.

The proximity of the two functions makes it all the more important to ensure that the segregation of duties is maintained at all times.

Answer to Question 2

> *'Describe the FX confirmation process, covering the reasons for sending confirmations, the advantages and disadvantages of the different methods of confirming and the control framework surrounding confirmations'.*

A confirmation is the record of the terms of a transaction that should be sent out by each party within one to three hours of trade time. The confirmation provides a necessary final check against dealing errors and should be independent of the trading room and be performed entirely by operations. Using data from the settlements and payments systems, the confirmations provide a check to ensure that the operations areas of each institution have recorded the same details for each transaction. For this reason, Reuters deal checks and trader call backs do not constitute a substitute for proper confirmations.

The confirmation should contain (at a minimum) details of the counterparties and location, broker (where appropriate), transaction date, value date, currency amounts (bought and sold), exchange rate and settlement instructions.

The most common forms of confirmation, from least preferable to most preferable, are by phone, mail, fax, telex, SWIFT. The electronic forms of transmission are preferable as they are faster. Of these, the use of the fax requires extra diligence because of the risks involved - i.e. fax is not a secure method.

Operations is responsible for checking inbound confirmations carefully upon receipt and for monitoring all unconfirmed transactions. Risk in the confirmation process arises either when discrepancies are missed or when trades are not confirmed. Standard escalation procedures should be in place to pursue and resolve discrepancies.

Answer to Question 3(a)

> *'Describe briefly . . .*
> *(a) netting'*

There are two types of netting, payment netting and close-out (credit) netting. Payment netting is the practice of combining all trades between two counterparties and calculating a single net payment in each currency for each value date. It may be conducted on a bilateral or multilateral basis. The establishment of payment netting between counterparties is useful in reducing settlement risk, operational risk and operational costs. FX Net is an example of a bi-lateral payment netting system.

Close-out netting relates to the final settlement of any unsettled contracts in the event of a counterparty default. This would result in a single net obligation (from the closing-out and netting of all unrealised gains and losses) that is either payable or receivable, thus removing the possibility of 'cherry-picking'. The operational process of payment netting should be supported by a legal agreement and legal opinions confirming enforceability in relevant jurisdictions. This agreement usually takes the form of a multi-page master agreement incorporating close-out netting. ECHO is a clearing house that supports multilateral payment and close-out netting.

Answer to Question 3(b)

> *'Describe briefly . . .*
> *(b) Nostro reconciliations'*

The nostro reconciliation occurs at the end of the trade settlement process to ensure a trade has settled properly and that all the expected cash flows have occurred. This involves a comparison of expected cash movements and actual cash movements both paid out and received by the nostro bank. The reconciliation should take place as soon as possible on value date and in no instance should it be done later than the day following settlement date. The process should be automated wherever possible. If any differences occur the operations must follow up with sales & trading and/or the counterparty to resolve the discrepancy. The cause of the discrepancy might be that wrong settlement or trade information was captured, or that the nostro bank made an error. In the event of late payment the culpable party would then arrange to pay with good value or pay compensation.

Answer to Question 3(c)

'Describe briefly . . .
(c) Collateral'

Collateral is an asset pledged to a counterparty, who has the right to apply it against any losses that it may incur if the party pledging the asset defaults. Collateralized trading is known as margin trading in certain markets. Typically, a collateral taker would require an initial margin and subsequent variation margin dependant upon the daily mark-to-market on both the collateral and the trading position supported. Use of collateralised trading may reduce credit (replacement and settlement) risk but it does not eliminate the need for a credit decision. A credit decision will have to be made on the type and amount of collateral required for each counterparty.

Similarly there are both legal (related to good title to the assets) and operational risks associated with the taking of collateral that have to be addressed. Collateralised trading has opened up various markets to smaller investors and asset/investment managers who may previously not have had such access owing to credit considerations.

Examples of commonly used collateralized trading facilities are: repo futures (margin) and FX.

Answer to Question 4

> *'Explain FX settlement risk and briefly outline the initiatives being taken to reduce this risk'.*

FX settlement risk is the risk that one party to an FX trade delivers the sold currency to the counterparty but does not receive the purchased currency from the counterparty.

The reduction of FX settlement risk is being actively pursued by the regulatory authorities following the publication, in March 1996, by the Bank for International Settlements of the report prepared by the Committee on Payment and Settlement Systems of the central banks of the Group of Ten countries. The initiatives being taken are:

1. Adoption of the best practice recommendations for measuring and managing FX settlement exposures.

2. Use of well-founded bilateral or multilateral netting schemes, such as FX Net and CLS.

3. The enhancement of national payment systems to incorporate real time gross settlement (RTGS).

4. The project set up by the 'Group of 20' banks to explore the feasibility of establishing a multi-currency settlement service to achieve PVP for FX settlements.

Answer to Question 5

> *'Explain real time gross settlement and briefly outline its benefits'.*

RTGS is the real time settlement of payments in central bank funds by means of direct postings to the settlement accounts of each of the settlement banks. The benefits are:

- The receipt of guaranteed funds and finality of settlement.

- The reduction in the possibility of the incidence of systemic risk.

- This provides the foundation stone for the implementation of DVP for securities settlements and PVP for FX settlements.

Answer to Question 6

> *'What are delivery versus payment (DVP) and payment versus delivery (PVP) and their benefits?'*

DVP is the simultaneous exchange of payment against the delivery of securities whereby good title passes against the receipt of guaranteed funds. The main benefit is:

- It eliminates the risk that one party to the transaction may default to the disadvantage of the other party, who has or will settle their side of the transaction, - i.e. if payment is made then the securities will be received and vice versa.

PVP is the simultaneous exchange of the two payments of an FX transaction with the delivery and receipt of guaranteed funds. The main benefit is:

- It eliminates the risk that one party to the transaction may default to the disadvantage of the other party, who has or will settle their side of the transaction, - i.e. if payment of the sold currency is made then the purchased currency will be received.

Answer to Question 7

> *'Describe the advantages of SSIs when compared with deal-by-deal exchange of instructions'.*

The main advantages are:

Security

By exchanging standard settlement instructions which are confirmed by authenticated SWIFT message, tested telex or letter bearing two verified authorised signatures, the risk of fraud is virtually eliminated.

Settlement risk

Where instructions are exchanged on a deal-by-deal basis, either by the traders or in the back offices, there is a risk of misunderstanding or misinterpretation of information as well as of transposition errors when keying the information into systems. These errors can result in serious financial losses in the form of overdraft interest claims as well as damage to relationships between counterparties when responsibility for such errors is disputed.

Processing efficiency

The use of SSIs provides the following savings/benefits:

-   It reduces time/effort of deal input.
-   it eliminates the requirement for back-office to swap instructions over the telephone.
-   It reduces the level of confirmation discrepancies and the associated time/effort in resolving them.
-   It enables greater level of automation, thereby reducing staff costs and exchange risk. (By speeding up the process of exchanging confirmations, errors may be detected and corrected earlier).

Answer to Question 8

> 'What are the benefits of using the central money office (CMO) to deliver sterling securities?'

During the boom of the 1980s it was decided that the increasing number of physical sterling negotiable paper being walked around the city was unacceptable. The Bank of England introduced a system whereby paper can be transferred through a system by book-entry transfer, the Central Moneymarkets Office (CMO) service.

Members of the service can now deliver large amounts of paper around the City within minutes in electronic form, rather than physically issuing the paper, getting each individual piece signed (normally twice), then requesting a member of staff (usually a messenger) to walk the paper, sometimes miles away, to the correct buyer.

The payments are automated. The seller enters a consideration amount which, on completion of the trade by the buyer, debits the buyer's account and credits the seller's account, thus saving costs by eliminating the need for bankers' payments, cheques, etc., and making the payment process quicker and more secure.

The delivery through CMO also decreases the chances of fraud and theft by restricting deliveries to members of the service and eliminating the movement and storage of the physical paper.

With physical paper the buyer has to check all signatures and store the paper, thus slowing the process and requiring the buyer to equip the office with strong rooms or safes. With CMO, the paper is managed at the Bank of England, thus these problems are avoided.

To sum up, CMO is:

- Quicker: delivery is not dependant on the availability of people to hand-deliver, as it is with physical paper.
- Safer: walking large numbers of CDs around London can be dangerous and open to theft or loss.
- More secure: physical paper has to be stored in large safe's, whereas non physical paper is held at the Bank of England.

III

CASE STUDIES

Case study 1

You receive your SWIFT statement from your USD correspondent, Citibank, New York, showing the following entries:

DEBITS

Amount	Ref	Value date
5,000,000.00	AIBLGB2L	961016
7,500,000.00	MIDIUS3 3	961015
9,247,500.00	OELBATWW	961016
10,000,000.00	MGTCFFPP	961016

CREDITS

Amount	Ref	Value date
1,001,447.50	CRLYGB2L	961016
8,567,600.00	DEUTDBFF	961016
10,000,000.00	RBCFXDEPTTOR	961016
25,000,000.00	BANK TOKYO	961016

Your general ledger for Citibank, New York, shows:

DEBITS

Amount	Ref	Value date
8,567,600.00	DEUTDEFF	961016
10,000,000.00	ROYLCATT	961016
10,014,475.00	CRLYGB2L	961016
25,000,000.00	BOFTJPJT	961016

CREDITS

Amount	Ref	Value date
5,000,000.00	ALLIEDIMSHLDN	961016
7,500,000.00	MIDIUS3 3	961016
9,247,500.00	OSTLAND WIEN	961016
10,000,000.00	MGTCFFPP	961016

1. How would you reconcile the above entries?
2. How would you resolve any discrepancies?

Case study 2

As the brokerage clerk, upon reconciling ABC Broker's monthly account, you discover that two trades which should have been net of brokerage have actually been included and charged on the invoice for a total of £847.50.

The monthly bill, after the application of a 30% discount, is for £10,470.60. Assuming that both deals are subsequently agreed as being net of brokerage, recalculate the amount of commission due to the broker.

Case study 3

A SWIFT MT202 payment order in respect of a JPY loan to Barclays Bank, London, has been sent to your nostro correspondent bank, Sumitomo, Tokyo, with the wrong value date, - i.e. value 17/10/96 when it should have been value 18/10/96.

It is now 17.00 hours on 17/10/96. What would be the best way to rectify the situation?

Case study 4

It is 17.00 hours. You, the reconciliations clerk, are the only person left in the back office. The late shift dealer upon checking the Reuters 2001 hard copy of deals concluded today discovers that there is a USD/JPY deal ticket that has not been written out for value tomorrow.

The deal is our sale of 5 yards of JPY (5,000,000,000). What could you do?

Case study 5

It is 15.20 hours when your MM dealers discover they are still £5,000,000 short. They can only cover their shortage by effecting a GBP/USD overnight swap (buy GBP, sell USD value today; sell GBP buy USD value tomorrow) with a London bank.

Assuming this course of action is agreed and taken, what action is necessary by the back office?

Case study 6

You are the confirmations clerk and have received a confirmation from BCI Milan re their purchase of JPY 10 yards value tomorrow. They have confirmed payment to Bank of Tokyo, Tokyo, but your SSI data base says 'Sumitomo, Tokyo'. What action should you take?

Answers to case study questions

Case study 1

1   You would mark off all ledger CRs and DRs that match exactly (in amount, beneficiary and value date) with the statement DRs and CRs.

2   To resolve the discrepancies - namely an apparent debit a day early for the USD 7,500,000 and the wrong statement CR of only USD 10,000,000 compared with your expected ledger DR of 10,014,750 - you would first need to obtain your original SWIFT messages to ensure they tally with the deal tickets. If they do not tally, then you would have to send amendments to Citibank.

Assuming they do tally, then you would need to contact Citibank to enquire why the USD 7,500,000 was debited a day early (and pre-advise them that you may need to claim for O/D charges if they cannot correct with good value).

For the shortfall on the CRLYGB2L deal, either Citibank have under-credited the account or Crédit Lyonnais, London, has sent the wrong instruction. (This could have been a deposit deal rolled over with interest and they have made it principal only).

Case study 2

£10,470.60 x $\frac{100}{70}$ = £14,958.00 - 847.50 = £14,110.50 x 70% = £9,877.35

Case study 3

Ideally, if Barclays Bank, London, also maintains its nostro at Sumitomo, then you could try to instruct the nostro bank to adjust the value (MT999 would suffice) in your own and the beneficiary's account from 17/10 to 18/10. However, they may say they need to contact Barclays first.

However, if Barclays Bank, London, held its JPY account elsewhere, then you will need to ask BARCGB2L for one day's use of funds to mitigate your debit interest incurred at Sumitomo, Tokyo.

Case study 4

Attempt to locate someone in your New York office (because of the time difference) who has the authority to execute the payment order on your behalf. Also, the dealer may need reminding that he may have a deal to cover (with accompanying risk) based on the movement in rates against the rate on deal now discovered. Dealers should also be reminded to do the deal check earlier. (As clerk, you should ensure the incident is reported to the head of the back office).

Case study 5

Ensure receipt of the £5 million by CHAPS before 3.30 pm or via Bank of England after 3.30 pm and before 4.30 pm. Ensure payment of the USD by MT202 value today. Check the sterling dealer has advised the USD dealer of the change to his/her position.

Case study 6

Check the actual confirmation. Based on what the confirmation says, refer the matter up and suggest pay according to the SSI received. Check with the SSI clerk to ascertain if there are any amended SSI instructions received recently from BCI. If time allows, revert direct to the counterparty to clarify the situation. Send SWIFT to advise what you have done, whether you have clarified the situation or not - MT399.

APPENDIX 1

▌▌▌

MARKET INTERACTIVITY

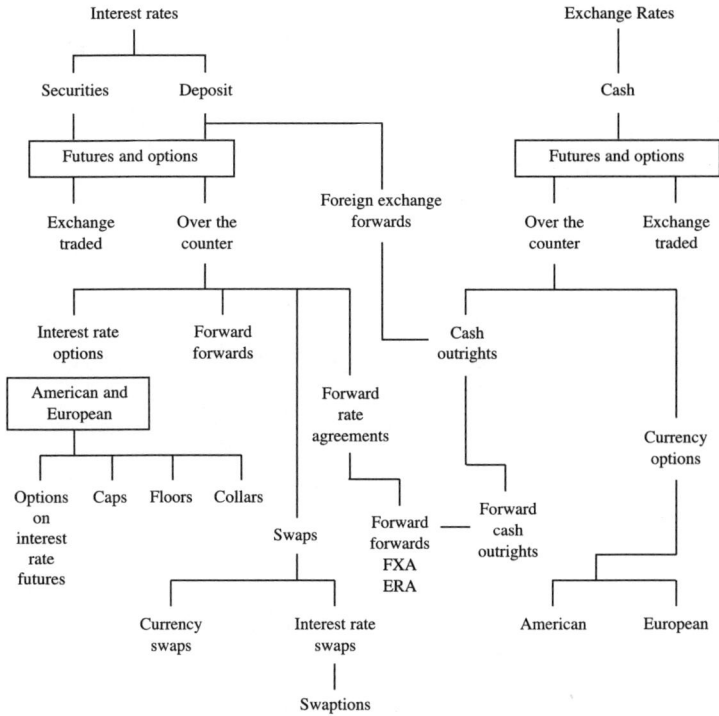

```
Interest rates                                    Exchange Rates
     |                                                  |
  ┌──┴──┐                                               |
Securities   Deposit                                   Cash
     |         |                                        |
┌────────────────────┐                        ┌───────────────────┐
│ Futures and options │                        │ Futures and options │
└────────────────────┘                        └───────────────────┘
     |         |          Foreign exchange          |         |
Exchange    Over the      forwards           Over the    Exchange
traded      counter                          counter      traded
     |         |                                  |         |
Interest rate  Forward              Cash
options        forwards           outrights
     |                                  
┌────────────────┐       Forward                        Currency
│ American and   │       rate                            options
│ European       │       agreements
└────────────────┘
  ┌──┬──┬──┬──┐
Options Caps Floors Collars            Forward    Forward
on                              Swaps  forwards   cash
interest                               FXA        outrights
rate                                   ERA
futures
     Currency     Interest rate              American   European
     swaps        swaps
                    |
                 Swaptions
```

181

APPENDIX 2

▌▌▌

MARKET AUTHORITIES/ DOCUMENTATION

IFEMA   **International Foreign Exchange Master Agreement**
Governs all FX deals up to 2 years

IFEOMA   **International Foreign Exchange & Options Master Agreement**
Same as IFEMA + options (not yet widely accepted)

ICOM   **International Currency Options Market**
Governs all option trades (previously know as LICOM)

FRABBA   **Forward Rate Agreement - British Bankers' Association**
FRA standard documentation

TBMA/ISMA   **The Bond Market Association/International Securities Market Association**

GMRA   **Global Master Repo Agreement**

European Repurchase Markets

BBAIRS   **British Bankers' Association Interest Rate Swaps**
Interest rate swap documentation

ISDA   **International Swap & Derivatives' Association**
Originally to replace BBAIRS but 1992 version onwards has documentation to cover options, FX, netting and often amended to cover FRA's etc.

APPENDIX 3

|||

AUTOMATED SYSTEMS

Society for Worldwide Interbank Financial Telecommunications (SWIFT)

Some SWIFT message types are:

MT000-099	System messages
MT100-199	Customer transfers, cheques
MT200-299	Financial institution transfers
MT300-399	FX, FX options, loans, deposits, FRAs, interest rate swaps
MT400-499	Collections, cash letters
MT500-599	Securities
MT600-699	Precious metals syndications
MT 700-799	Documentary credits, guarantees
MT800-899	Traveller's cheques
MT900-999	Balance reporting, rate changes, nostro statements, bilateral key exchange, netting, status enquiry.

Automated Confirmation System (ACS)

This is the system into which brokers send deal details. Banks Automated Confirmation Reception Terminal (BART) is the bank's software equivalent and then Transaction Automatic Matching (TRAM) matches up what the brokers send and the banks have to find any exceptions. Major users of these facilities thus avoid the need to actually send 'paper' confirmations to their counterparties.

BART

BART is a PC-based system, established in 1986, which provides a single point of control for your transactions. The main features are:

- Full audit controls - In-built audit facilities ensure that all received messages are automatically logged with date, time-stamp and sequence number to help you keep track of all transactions received and processed.

- Fast access to information - You can gain instant access to received data, whether for enquiry purposes, sorting or printing. Archive material can be retrieved within seconds and management reports automatically generated and distributed to other departments.

- Integrated treasury support - Automatic and seamless interfaces can link BART to your other systems such as those providing payment control, confirmation matching and brokerage management, thereby ensuring maximum benefit from the system.

The specific BART benefits are:

- Reduced risk of financial loss
- Increased security
- Improved processing efficiency
- Time saved on investigations

TRAM

This system can handle confirmations for foreign exchange or money market transactions, including CDs, FRAs and FX options, and can carry out the matching process against the details held in your in-house system against counterparty, broker or corporate confirmations whether received via SWIFT, ACS, Reuters or EBS and is thus 'real-time' - confirmations received by mail or telex are allowed for with only minimal entries required.

The system classifies the degree of matching as follows:

- *Paired* - all details match.

- *Proposed pair* - most details match but a visual check is required to allow/disallow the match.

- *Close fit* - confirmations differ in one or more of the mandatory fields (rate, amount, value date).

- *Time out* - here TRAM has not been able to find a match within a specified time limit and it needs to be investigated.

Management information is available initially in the form of a status screen which summarises the number of confirmations received from each source and their current matching status. Also, other reports can be optionally obtained to highlight increases/decreases in volume for a particular type, differences in matching rates between types, etc. The following other specific optional modules are available:

- *Feedback*: This module ensures the status of deals, matched or otherwise, and is updated in the bank's in-house system, thereby ensuring that payments are not released until matching is perfect.

- *Chaser letters/SWIFT chasers*: According to a bank's own definition of overdue, the system can produce a chaser letter which, where SWIFT chaser letter is implemented, will then be automatically sent out via SWIFT.

- *Automated time out management system (ATOM)*: This enhancement automatically sets and updates the time out values per counterparty. This then affords proactive management of potential losses should late confirmations be received.

The specific benefits of TRAM are:

- Reduced settlement errors and related costs
- Increased productivity
- Faster matching
- Greater staff motivation
- Up-to-the-moment management information

Clearing House Automated Payments System (CHAPS)

This is a UK clearing system for large credit transfers. It has 14 member banks including the Bank of England. It settles on a multilateral basis at the end of each day and accounts for 92% of the value of total transactions.

Clearing House Interbank Payments System (CHIPS)

This is owned by the New York Clearing House Association. It settles payments multilaterally at the end of the day and has 122 participating banks (Edge Act banks, investment companies and commercial banks).

APPENDIX 4

III

SETTLEMENT OF TRANSACTIONS IN THE INTERNATIONAL SECURITIES MARKET

Euroclear and Clearstream are the two major depositories and settlement organisations in the international securities market. However, both institutions also accept and settle transactions involving domestic securities. Their combined turnover in 1992 amounted to USD 14.5 trillion, or roughly USD 55 billion on average per business day. Clearstream was established in 1970. It handles 38 currencies, 33 markets and 80 countries. Its USD turnover is 100 billion per day. Currently there is no bridge between Clearstream and Euroclear. Euroclear was established in 1968. It handles over 100,000 different securities in 30 markets (mostly domestic) in 35 currencies. Its turnover in all currencies for the third quarter of 1998 was a total of the USD equivalent of 12.45 trillion, which equated to approximately USD 4.7 trillion per month or 200 billion per day.

The international securities market

The international securities market consists of a number of segments which have their own characteristics. They include the international bond market for long-term debt instruments (Euro-bonds and foreign bonds)*

---

* Foreign bonds are issued in domestic capital markets by non-resident borrowers and underwritten and sold by a syndicate composed of institutions located in the country in which the bonds are offered (which may, however, include subsidiaries of multinational financial institutions. Euro-bonds are usually issued simultaneously in several capital markets and underwritten by an international syndicate (they are almost wholly exempt from disclosure and registration requirements and from withholding taxes). However the distinction between Euro-bonds and foreign bonds has become increasingly blurred.

and the Euro-note market, where short-term paper such as commercial securities market is a multi-currency market; by far the largest proportion of the stock of international bonds is denominated in US dollars (USD 680 billion in 1992) with other currencies trailing well behind.

Since, in many countries, institutional investors are prohibited from buying unlisted securities, most international bonds are listed on established stock exchanges to improve their marketability. This is done, most commonly, on the Luxembourg Stock Exchange and the London Stock Exchange. Trading, however, is normally done over-the-counter and conducted by various specialised dealer groups. One particular feature of the international securities market is that most of the securities (especially in the Euro-markets) are in bearer form and are not fully dematerialised. In principle, the transfer of ownership can then take place through book-entry in these security accounts. Furthermore, by simultaneously holding cash deposits with Euroclear and Clearstream, users can also let the cash leg of the securities transactions be settled by these organisations. As a result, Euroclear and Clearstream can be defined as both securities and large-value funds transfer systems.

Institutional characteristics

The Euroclear system is operated by Morgan Guaranty, Brussels, through a separate administrative unit called the Euroclear Operations Centre, under an operating agreement with the Euroclear Clearance System, *Société Coopérative*, set up under Belgian law. The Coopérative, in turn, is controlled partly by a large number of participants in the system (11.5% of its share capital) and by the UK-based Euroclear Clearance System Public Limited Company (88.5%). The latter company, which actually owns the system, is owned by 124 banks, brokers and investment institutions. Centrale de Livraison de Valeurs Mobilières (Clearstream), société anonyme (SA) is a Luxembourg-based limited company which provides, in return for payment, for the circulation, custody and management of securities (and precious metals). It is currently owned by 108 shareholding financial institutions from some 20 different companies. Both institutions have customers or participants comprising major banks or security companies (about 2,500 each) in a large number of companies.* Reflecting the 'cooperative approach' taken by the owners of both the Euroclear and Clearstream systems, no institution is

---

* They include a number of central banks and official institutions.

entitled to hold more than a small fraction (3.25% and 5% respectively) of the shares in these companies.

Euroclear and Clearstream operate as international securities depositories. They do not hold the securities in custody themselves but rely on a worldwide network of depository banks. The custody services offered by the depositories include storing the issue in the vault, administration of coupon, dividend and redemption payments, related tax services, and the exercise of warrants, conversion and other options. To limit physical movements of securities and enhance security, each individual issue is deposited and immobilised with only one depository; in the case of Euro-bonds this is normally the paying agent for the issue. Typically, the deposited securities become fully fungible, which means that the owner no longer has title to a security with a particular registration number but receives a claim on the pool of securities held by the settlement organisations; the transfer of ownership takes place by book-entry in the securities accounts with Euroclear and Clearstream.

Apart from custody and settlement services, Euroclear and Clearstream offer their customers various other services, including trade matching and confirmation, cash management and financing facilities, proprietary telecommunications systems, and securities lending and borrowing programmes. Regarding funds transfer facilities, participants pay and receive funds in the different currencies accepted by the systems through each system's cash correspondent in the respective country of issue.

Settlements procedures

The settlement procedures followed by Euroclear and Clearstream are similar and can be summarised in four points. Firstly, both institutions operate a gross securities and cash settlement system: each instruction is carried out individually with the crediting/debiting of securities accounts taking place simultaneously with the corresponding debiting/crediting of the cash accounts. However, the instructions are not carried out on a continuous basis but are stored by the computer up to a certain cut-off time, after which they enter an automated batch settlement programme. All validated and matched settlement instructions enter the settlement process, which is carried out during the night prior to the settlement date.*

---

* Until September 1993, Cedel, processed, validated and matched instructions in the afternoon on the settlement day. It continues to run a daytime settlement process. Euroclear has announced that it will also introduce a daytime settlement process.

Secondly, securities transfers and the related payments are executed on a delivery against payment principle. This means that the settlement of individual transactions is successfully completed only if the selling participant has sufficient securities in his securities account or has access to securities borrowing facilities to permit delivery and if the buyer has a sufficient cash or cash credit position available for payment. Once the settlement programme is terminated, settlement is final and participants are notified of their securities and cash positions. The strict application of the principle means that a number of instructions entering the automated settlement process are not executed. They normally re-enter the settlement process on the following business day.

Thirdly, delivery instructions are not processed in the chronological order in which they are transmitted by the participants but according to a certain rank for each individual issue. The ranking criteria differ between Euroclear and Clearstream but include the priority codes given by the participants themselves, the settlement date (normally old instructions before more recent ones) and the nominal amount of the transaction. The automated settlement process groups all trades related to the same issue and subsequently attempts to settle as many trades as possible for each issue using a so called 'chaining' procedure. Very often settlement instructions reflect the fact that the same security has been bought and sold through one or more intermediaries (brokers) a number of times during the trading day. The computer program will, for instance, try to recognise so-called back-to-back transactions involving the purchase and sale by two participants of the same security through a broker and treat such transactions as a group for settlement purposes. The chaining program also tries to settle as many transactions as possible related to the same security in light of the cash and security positions available in the participant's accounts and by taking account of the expected movements in the accounts during the settlement processing style. These patterns of settlement are optimised by recourse to recursive simulations.

Fourthly, since many trades in the international securities market will be conducted by counterparties belonging to the other settlement system, Euroclear and Clearstream have automated the linkage between their securities settlements by installing an electronic 'bridge'. Cross-system settlement is thus also handled by book-entry transfers between the two systems. For this, each system maintains a securities and a cash account with the other. When one of the two organisations finds itself with a substantial custody holding for the other, the two systems transfer securities from one system's depository to the other system's depository.

In contrast, cash settlements between the two systems take place on a net basis for each individual currency each day. Given that the volume of securities between the two systems results in substantial cash movements as well, each system has arranged a special credit line for the other to cover the inter-system credit exposures.

In order to enable participants to settle transactions in domestic markets through the international settlement systems, Euroclear and Clearstream provide two types of linkages to domestic clearing systems. In the case of direct links, Euroclear and Clearstream themselves hold an account with a local clearing system and cross-border transactions can be settled without the intervention of the local depository. Where there is no direct link, a local Euroclear/Clearstream depository holds an account with its domestic clearing system and trades between Euroclear and Clearstream participants and their counterparties in the domestic market are settled through the intermediary of this depository.

Other features (liquidity facilities and risk management)

With respect to risk management in both the Euroclear and the Clearstream systems, principal risk is limited by the delivery against payment principle used by both organisations, while liquidity risk is reduced by various cash credit facilities and securities lending programmes. Moreover, the combined exposure for each participant under both these lending schemes must normally be collateralised by holdings of securities (expressed in US dollars). For this, the value of the securities eligible as collateral is marked to market each day and adjustments are made taking into account the type of instrument and the exchange rate of the respective currency of issue vis-à-vis the dollar. With respect to the credit line which Euroclear and Clearstream have opened for one another to cover the execution of 'bridge' settlements, this facility is covered by a letter of credit which each system obtains from a separate syndicate of banks.

Central banks are not directly involved in providing payment services for the settlement of international securities transactions. The link with the respective domestic payment systems is through the participation of Euroclear's/Clearstream's cash correspondents in the respective local interbank funds transfer systems. Various central banks have a relationship with one or both of the international clearing organisations, however, through the direct or indirect linkage which these systems have with a number of domestic securities settlement systems. For example, Euroclear and Clearstream have links with the Banque de France for the settlement of transactions in various domestic government securities, with the Bank of England (for ECU treasury bills), the Nederlandsche Bank (for Euro-commercial paper) and with the National Bank of Belgium.

APPENDIX 5

█ █ █

REAL TIME GROSS SETTLEMENT (RTGS) VIA CONTINUOUS LINKED SETTLEMENT (CLS)

One way to reduce settlement risk has been the use of 'netting' in all its various forms - bilateral via systems like Citinet, multilateral like ECHO or Multinet. Following the Allsopp Report (March 1996) requiring:

• action by individual banks to control their FX settlement exposures
• collective industry action to provide multi-currency services to reduce risk
• action by central banks to support and encourage private sector progress

the subsequent action by the Group of 20 (G20) in investigating the optimum way of reducing risk led to the establishment of CLS Services (CLSS) after the feasibility of running continuous-linked settlement was approved. In December 1997 CLSS acquired the share capital of both ECHO and the Multinet International Bank and, at September 1998, there were 60 shareholders from 14 countries.

Payment (across CLS's banks with central banks') bank	- Members pay the CLS bank in their short currencies - Members receive payment from the CLS in their long currencies

Settlement (across member's accounts on CLS bank books)	CLS bank - posts incoming funds from members - settles transactions - pays out settlement proceeds to members

A pay-in schedule for a settlement bank:

	Net	Payment due by CET (cumulative amount)				
	Position	8:00	9:00	10:00	11:00	12:00
USD	+100					
EUR	-500	100	200	300	400	500
JPY	-1,050	250	500	750	1,000	
GBP	+300					
CHF	-1,000	200	400	600	800	1,000
CAD	+300					

The CLS bank will have settlement with funding through automated systems:

The following diagram shows the interrelationship of all participants in continuous linked settlement:

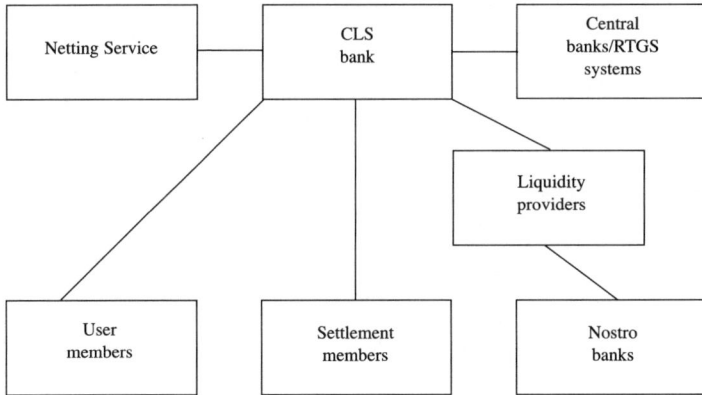

An example of how 'maximum partial settlement' works:

	Member X				Member Y			
	Payment due	Cash balance	Limit	Amount payable	Payment	Cash due	Limit balance	Amount payable
USD	100	200	-500	100				
EUR					120	500	-500	120
JPY	100	-300	-300	0				
GBP					100	0	-300	100
CHF	100	-250	-3000	50				
CAD					100	200	-200	100
Total	**300**			**150**	**320**			**320**

Member X can only make payments up to 150, whereas Member Y can make payments up to the full amount payable.

Service suspended since 15 May 1999, finally came into force - but not in final format - in September 2002

APPENDIX 6

███

REPO SETTLEMENTS

Sell/buy back

Example 1

The repo

Trade date	8 November 1996
Settlement date	12 November 1996
Maturity date	12 December 1996
Term	30 days
Repo rate	5.25% pa (Actual/360)

The collateral

The bond	GEC 7.00 5/99
Maturity	4 May 1999
On settlement date	188 day's interest accrued
Clean price	102.25
Accrued interest	$\frac{188}{360} \times 7.00 = 3.6556$
Dirty price	102.25+3.6556=105.9056

Example 2

The repo

Trade date	8 November 1996
Settlement date	12 November 1996
Maturity date	12 December 1996
Term	30 days
Repo rate	5.25% pa (Actual/360)

The collateral

The bond	GEC 5.50 12/98
Maturity	11 December 1998
On settlement date	359 day's interest accrued
Clean price	99.50
Accrued interest	$\frac{359}{360} \times 5.50 = 5.4847$
Dirty price	99.50 + 5.4847 = 104.9847

Example 3

A dealer sells USD 1,000,000 of T-bonds for 7 days. The bonds have 273 days of accrued interest due on spot date, and current market clean price is 100.28. The settlement amount is therefore the full 'dirty' price of the bond:

Clean amount	USD	1,002,800.00
Accrued interest (273/360 x 6.5% x 1 mio)	USD	49,292.67
Settlement amount (dirty price)	USD	1,052,091.67

The repurchase amount depends on the agreed repo rate of interest. If we suppose it was 5.0625%, the interest paid on the dirty amount is thus:

Repo interest (5.0625% x 7/360 x 1,052,091.67	USD	1,035.65
Investor pays in total 1,052,091.67+1,035.65	USD	1,053,127.32

The forward repurchase price then has to be adjusted for the difference between the repo interest due and the accrued interest over the period:

Repo interest (5.0625 x 7/360)	USD	1,035.65
Less accrued (6.5% x 7/360)	USD	1,263.89
Difference (on USD 1 mio nominal)		-228.24

Expressed per USD 100 nominal = -0.022824 (USD)
Thus the repurchase price becomes 100.28 - 0.022824 = 100.257176

Another way to calculate this is:

Investor (buyer) repays	USD	1,053,127.32
after allowing for accrued interest and interest		
on that (49,291.67 + 1,263.89)	USD	50,555.56
	USD	1,002,571.76

i.e. a 'price' of 100.257176

Classic repo

Example 1 - without margin requirement

Settlement date

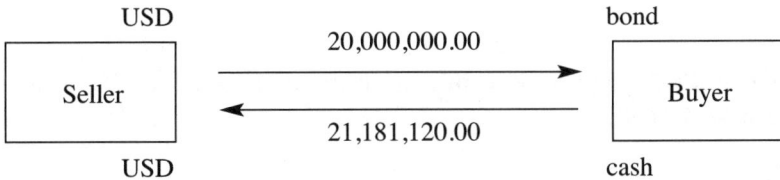

at a dirty price of 105.9056

Maturity date

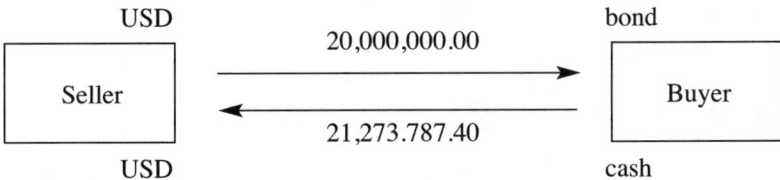

Calculation of repo interest:

$$\frac{21,181,120.00 \times 5.25 \times 30}{360 \times 100} \quad = \quad 92,667.40$$

Total amount to be paid at maturity:

$$21,181,200.00 + 92,667.40 \quad = \quad 21,273,787.40$$

With margin requirement (haircut) of 2%

The process would be the same except that the cash amount would be worked out on a bond price that would be calculated as follows:

$$\frac{105.9056 \times 100}{102.00} \quad = \quad 103.8290196$$

This would produce a cash amount of:

$$\frac{103.8290196 \times 20,000,000.00}{100.00} \quad = \quad 20,765,803.92$$

The repo would be calculated in the same way.

Example 2 - with a margin requirement (haircut) of 2% and a margin call

Settlement date

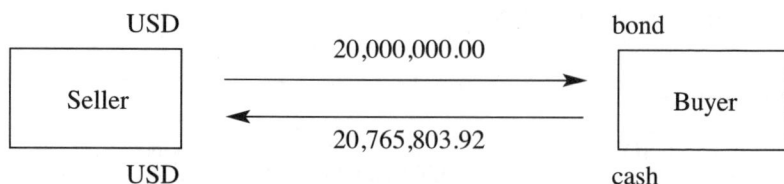

$$\text{USD} \qquad\qquad\qquad\qquad \text{bond}$$

Seller → 20,000,000.00 → Buyer

← 20,765,803.92

$$\text{USD} \qquad\qquad\qquad\qquad \text{cash}$$

At a price of $\dfrac{105.9056 \times 100}{102} \quad = \quad 103.8290196$

Maturity date

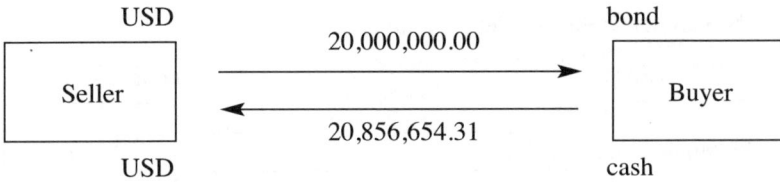

Calculation of repo interest:

$$\frac{20,765,803.92 \times 5.25 \times 30}{360 \times 100} \quad = \quad 90,850.39$$

Total amount to be paid at maturity:

$$20,765,803.92 + 90,850.39 \quad = \quad 20,856.654.31$$

If, on 18 November 1996, the price of the bond fell to 100.50 then the amount of the security would have to be recalculated as follows:

Clean price: 100.5000

Accrued interest: $\dfrac{194 \times 7,00}{360.00} = 3.7722222$

Dirty price: 104.2722

Impact of haircut: $\dfrac{104.2722222 \times 100}{102.00} = 102.2276688$

Required security: original cash amount $= \dfrac{20,765,803.92 \times 100}{102.2276688}$

$$= 20,313,291..07$$

If the bond is available in amount of USD 1,000.00 then the seller would have to put up additional collateral of USD 314,000.00.

The relevant transfers that would subsequently take place are as follows:

18 November 1996 - settlement date

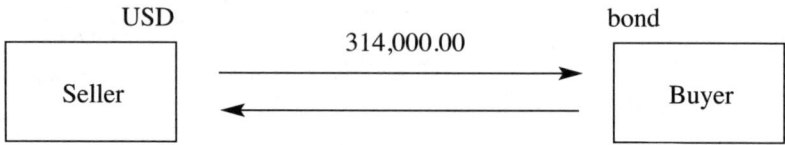

USD		bond
	314,000.00 →	
Seller	←	Buyer

Maturity date

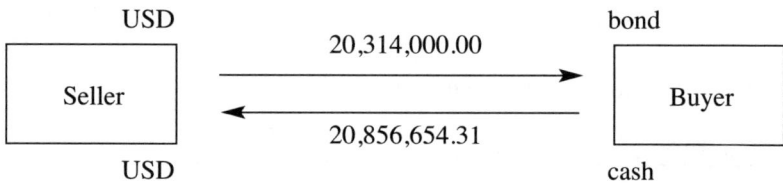

USD		bond
	20,314,000.00 →	
Seller	←	Buyer
	20,856,654.31	
USD		cash

APPENDIX 7

III

THE KEY ATTRACTIONS OF CHAPS EURO

The CHAPS board is raising the profile of the CHAPS euro system and actively marketing the service which it will provide. Copies are available by e-mail from: sm.chapseuro@apacs.org.uk. The CHAPS board is now drawing attention to the fact that CHAPS euro is based on the same concept as, and will sit alongside, the present CHAPS sterling service which is widely understood and appreciated.

The CHAPS Company's aim is to provide a euro service at least as good as the CHAPS sterling service. CHAPS euro's twin purposes are:

- To be a stand-alone real time gross settlement (RTGS) system based in London.

- To be the UK's access route to TARGET.

Because of the scale of euro activity expected to take place in UK financial markets, the stand-alone role of CHAPS euro will be very important.

The major attractive features of CHAPS euro are as follows:

It is a riskless system: As with CHAPS sterling, CHAPS euro will be a true RTGS system, with each payment settled immediately in real-time at the Bank of England. So intraday finality is provided and settlement risk eliminated.

CHAPS has a proven capacity to undertake major developments: In total, the CHAPS Company has a 14-year track record of providing a high quality payment service combined with a robust system. In 1996, the CHAPS Company, in partnership with the Bank of England, transformed the UK sterling wholesale payment system from an end-of-day net settlement system to an RTGS system. This project was successfully completed on schedule, without in any way affecting end-users or causing any diminution to the service provided. The development of a parallel euro system is, by comparison, relatively straightforward.

Resilient and robust in handling high volumes: The CHAPS sterling RTGS system has been resilient and robust, operating without hitch since its inception over two years ago. It is the largest RTGS system in Europe, and second in the world only to Fedwire in the USA. On a peak day CHAPS has handled 135,000 payments with a value of £240 billion. Although CHAPS euro is being planned on the basis of initial traffic considerably lower than for CHAPS sterling, the RTGS processor will be capable of handling whatever volumes are required, without reducing the efficiency of the service, by adding capacity.

Broad geographic coverage: The CHAPS euro system includes a database showing all the CHAPS euro addressable bank identifier codes (BICs). Ultimately there are likely to be 20,000 BICs, including both UK and foreign bank addresses. Any bank will thus be able to use the database to route payments automatically to a wide range of destinations using straight-through processing, with an excellent level of recipient bank service.

Easy access via SWIFT: Rather than using a proprietary system, CHAPS euro is based on the SWIFT Fin Copy product, which enables low cost connections to the service to be made from anywhere in the world. So CHAPS euro will combine the experience, quality and resilience of CHAPS sterling with the ease of access of SWIFT.

Fast and efficient: CHAPS works as a high-speed system with minimal delays to payments. Once a sending bank releases a payment, the average time taken for it to reach a receiving bank is less than one minute, which compares favourably with any other European payment system. This is of great value to banks and their customers for time-critical payments.

Liquidity efficiency: As with CHAPS sterling, the CHAPS euro system has been designed to ensure liquidity efficiency, which is achieved through careful liquidity management and scheduling of payments by members. CHAPS uses the minimum liquidity necessary to ensure that payments experience little or no delay awaiting capacity. This allows CHAPS members to provide their customers with a highly efficient service.

Well understood operational rules: The CHAPS community has sound and well understood operational rules. Service level agreements ensure discipline in the CHAPS system whilst at the same time providing that member performance does not impact adversely on end-user customers. A smooth flow of payments is brought about by guidelines on members which determine payment volumes through the system at various points during the day. Under CHAPS end-to-end service levels and agreements, a sending member knows the service level it offers to customers. Customers must be credited on a same-day basis by recipient banks. The full amount of each payment is always credited to the customer's account.

Open all hours: The CHAPS Board has confirmed that CHAPS euro will be open on every day that TARGET is open and for the full operating hours each day (i.e. 07.00 to 18.00 CET for banks and 07.00 to 17.00 CET for customers).

Competitive in price: CHAPS euro will be priced competitively against other major euro payment systems. As it has a large database of automatically-addressable banks, there will be significantly reduced manual intervention. As a result, the overall cost of settling CHAPS euro will be less than for systems with fewer members and participants.

CHAPS is managed by banks taking into account their commercial needs: CHAPS is a member-owned and directed system which allows it to develop in ways which its members wish, in order to meet their needs. Members control their own payment flow in CHAPS. It will not be compulsory to schedule payments within CHAPS euro, and the decision about how and when to make payments is within member's control rather than decided by any third party. Sending banks know precisely where payments are in the end-to-end process at all times, and each member knows the position of its settlement account at the Bank of England through on-line links. Tried and trusted procedures are also in place to avoid member's balances falling below zero at the end of the day.

Operational and technical support: CHAPS provides its members with a full range of operational and technical support, including support in contingency situations and a rapid response to any problems which might arise.

Fully tested, giving absolute confidence in CHAPS euro's reliability: The CHAPS euro system underwent a comprehensive testing programme which to offer a strong degree of confidence in its availability, reliability, and integrity in the euro environment. All members have participated in group testing within CHAPS euro, and the Bank of England has sent payment messages across TARGET Interlinking to central banks in other countries. Integrated systems testing of all components of CHAPS euro and the linkages to TARGET, including central bank systems, were completed in time for the planned launch on the 4th January 1999.

APPENDIX 8

▌▌▌

DEPOSITORY AND CLEARING FACILITIES (DCC) AT BANK ONE, NA, LONDON

The Depository and Clearing Centre (DCC) was established as part of Bank One in 1976 as a clearing system for moneymarket instruments traded in London, and is a centralised settlement and custody service for a variety of financial instruments in all major trading currencies. The DCC started clearing Certificates of Deposit (CDs), and later diversified into clearing Euro and Sterling Commercial Paper (CP). During the 1980s, the DCC expanded its range of services by offering a full range of global corporate trust services to its clients.

The DCC is a direct member of the Central Moneymarkets Office (CMO) and Euroclear, and can settle clients' trades through the CMO and Euroclear systems. The DCC provides services to approximately 400 of the largest financial institutions, brokers, investors and their custodians in Europe. As the majority of active market participants are members, Bank One's clients benefit from the synergies of having the majority of counterparties in one place.

Maximising the Benefits of the London Money Market

London has been a global financial centre for over 200 years and is one of the world's most active, economic communities. This is illustrated by London's CD market which is large, in excess of 410 billion (USD), and very liquid. Whilst 55 percent of this is in Sterling-denominated CDs, the remainder is represented by multicurrency issuances, including USD, EUR, CAD, AUD and JPY. Recognising the ongoing requirement of a central counterparty for London's money market, the DCC continues to provide Agency, Clearing and Custodial services for the following products:

• All Internationally-cleared Instruments;

• Bank-to-Bank Bills;

• Bills of Exchange;

• DTC Eligible Equities;

• Euro Commercial Paper (ECP);

• Gilts;

• London CDs;

• Non-London CDs; and

• Treasury Bills.

Custody and Settlement

The DCC provides custody and settlement services for a multitude of instruments - CDs, Commercial Paper, Treasury Bills, Bills of Exchange and all internationally-cleared instruments tradeable within Euroclear. Key benefits off the DCC include:

• Majority of market participants are under one roof;

• Delivery versus Payment (DVP) and assured payment;

• Working with market professionals;

• Rapid account opening; and

• Comprehensive range of products serviced.

London CDs are the most actively settled instrument within the DCC, with 90 percent of USD CD trades in London settling in or via the DCC. The DCC is also a significant player in the highly liquid ECP market-settling over 50 ECP trades daily both internally within the DCC, Euroclear and Clearstream, as well as utilising DVP settlement links.

CD Issuing and Paying

As the leading clearer of physical CDs in the London market, the DCC also enjoys a pre-eminent position as the market leader for the issuance of CDs. DCC client,receive:

• Integration that allows for DVP settlement;

• CDs that deliver major cost savings;

• Alleviated burden of legal costs;

• Rapid implementation; and

• The opportunity of working with London's top CD IPA.

As a leading Issuing and Paying Agent, (IPA) we recognise that you need flexibility, experience and vision from all of your service providers. Bank One is at the forefront of product development - that contributes to DCC's success as well as the innovation that is associated with our CD IPA product.

Thanks to our considerable client base, we are able to pass onto our clients the economies of scale we realise. As many physical CD's do not leave the DCC vault area and since we settle over 90 percent of all USD CD trades, we are able to offer all our clients - both issuers and investors - an efficient, integrated service. Combined with our Standard Definitive CDs, this presents Issuers with considerable cost savings.

Standard Definitive CDs, standard blank CDs that Bank One provides in BBA - approved form and denomination - are overprinted only at issuance with the pre-agreed details for each client. These CDs are currently available in USD, EUR, CHF, JPY, AUD, CAD, HKD and some legacy currencies. This eliminates the need for the issuer to provide stock, thus leading to significant cost savings.

Bank One provides standard documentation to facilitate CD IPA business. We also negotiate documents in-house - alleviating the burden of legal costs and also significantly reducing the implementation time to ensure you can start issuing in weeks rather than months.

Assisting London Equity Markets With Access to the U.S.

The DCC is in the unique position of being the only Depository Trust Company (DTC) Lodgement Facility outside North America. Via an electronic link, we areable to effect immediate delivery of physical DTC eligible instruments to DTC accounts. Given Crest's new links with DTC, this service enables participants to rapidly deposit equities into DTC accounts, thus allowing onward trading within Crest and providing Crest clients with access to a fast, efficient lodgement process.

APPENDIX 9

III

EBA - EURO 1 OPERATION

Processing payments and queue management

Payment messages sent by participants for the purpose of being processed in EURO1 must carry the tag **'EBA' in field 103** of the message header. Messages with this tag are partially copied to the clearing computer via SWIFT's FIN-Copy service.

Payment messages are processed on an individual basis. Processing consists of checking the sending and the receiving participant's position and, if possible, adjusting their position. Should the adjustment lead to a **breach** of the sending participant's **debit cap** or the receiving participant's **credit cap**, the payment message would not be processed, but **put into an on-hold queue**.

Upon processing of a payment message, the clearing computer generates a release message to the FIN-Copy service and the original payment message is forwarded to the receiving participant. The system revisits a participant's on-hold queue each time a payment message in relation to that bank is processed to check whether the adjusted position allows for further processing of payment messages that are held in the participant's on-hold queue. To that effect, **the system follows the principle of 'by-passing FIFO'.**

A payment message can be cancelled by the sending participant as long as it is not processed.

Operational use of SWIFT identity

The EURO1 system is based on an information messaging infrastructure provided by SWIFT (Society for Worldwide Interbank Financial Telecommunication) using SWIFT message standards.

The system permits a participant to be identified by a 6, 8 or 11 character SWIFT BIC.

The design of the system allows for the use of up to 99 sub-addresses to enable multiple entry points by individual banks and their branches or subsidiaries for their payment messages without any modification to the system.

Message types available to Banks

The current system processes **MT100, MT102, MT103, MT202** and **MT400** messages. Payment messages can be sent five settlement days ahead of value date.

Timing of processing

The processing of the system **starts at 7:30 CET. Cut-off time** stands presently at **16:00 CET**.

Information management

Each participant has a workstation with a client-server capability that provides relevant information including:

- a position report showing the participant's current limits, balance and the total queued payments (if any) at any time during the day;

- certain payment details of payment messages queued in the central system - both sent and to be received;

- balance reports (at reporting time or intraday) and clearing statements (after cut-off time) for processed and held-over payment messages;

- pre-advice statements providing partial details of individual payment messages for future value.

EURO1's settlement service provider is the European Central Bank

The current cut-off time for sending payment messages is set at 16:00 CET. This enables all participants to have sufficient time to complete the settlement process for sending and receiving payments prior to TARGET's (Trans-European Automated Real-Time Gross Settlement Express Transfer System) closing time of 18:00 CET.

Settlement process

1. At cut-off time, SWIFT completes the processing of payment messages sent before cut-off, and informs each participant of the amount of its balance as results from all processed payment messages. Simultaneously, SWIFT sends the list of final balances to the EBA and the ECB.

2. In a first round, each participant with a debit balance (short participant) sends a payment instruction to its National Central Bank (NCB) in favour of the system's settlement account at the ECB.

3. The NCBs debit the accounts of the short participants and send payments via TARGET to the ECB.

4. The ECB credits the payments received to the settlement account and advises EBA Clearing accordingly.

5. Upon receipt of all payments due by short participants, EBA Clearing sends instructions to the ECB to transfer to each participant with a credit balance (long participant) an amount equivalent to its credit balance.

6. The ECB debits the settlement account according to the instructions received from EBA Clearing and generates a payment via TARGET to the NCB of each long participant.

7. The NCBs credit the accounts of the long participant and in return send a confirmation to the ECB.

8. The ECB forwards the confirmations to EBA Clearing.

9. Upon receipt of all confirmations, EBA Clearing notifies all participants that the settlement operations are completed.

10. At cut-off time, SWIFT completes the processing of payment messages sent before cut-off, and informs each participant of the amount

of its balance as results from all processed payment messages. Simultaneously, SWIFT sends the list of final balances to the EBA and the ECB.

11. In a first round, each participant with a debit balance (short participant) sends a payment instruction to its National Central Bank (NCB) in favour of the system's settlement account at the ECB.

12. The NCBs debit the accounts of the short participants and send payments via TARGET to the ECB.

13. The ECB credits the payments received to the settlement account and advises EBA Clearing accordingly.

14. Upon receipt of all payments due by short participants, EBA Clearing sends instructions to the ECB to transfer to each participant with a credit balance (long participant) an amount equivalent to its credit balance.

15. The ECB debits the settlement account according to the instructions received from EBA Clearing and generates a payment via TARGET to the NCB of each long participant.

16. The NCBs credit the accounts of the long participant and in return send a confirmation to the ECB.

17. The ECB forwards the confirmations to EBA Clearing.

18. Upon receipt of all confirmations, EBA Clearing notifies all participants that the settlement operations are completed.

The EURO1 system takes advantage of an innovative legal structure, the ' Single Obligation Structure'.

It has been established in accordance with the regulatory requirements as apply to large value net settlement system that the Single Obligation Structure provides a sound legal basis for the system.

The Single Obligation Structure achieves that the legal definition of the rights and obligations of the participants as result from the sending and receiving of payment messages reflects the manner in which the system actually functions.

The participants agree that their rights and obligations resulting from the sending and receiving of payment messages are, from the

outset, on a net basis. At any time on any given settlement day, there will only be one single amount payable by or to each participant. At no time gross obligations will arise in respect of payment messages.

The single amount owed by or to a participant automatically changes upon processing of each payment message sent or received by such participant. From the moment the first payment message is processed until settlement of the relevant amount, each participant has a single obligation (in the case of a negative amount) or a single claim (in the case of a positive amount) towards all other participants. The single obligation or claim is valid and enforceable at each and any time throughout the settlement day.

The Single Obligation Structure hence also does not allow for an unwind. Payment messages are **irrevocable and final upon being processed.**

The legal basis and the liquidity and loss sharing arrangements underpinning the system allow certainty of daily settlement and, accordingly, significantly limit potential systemic risk.

EBA Clearing has devised, together with the ECB, SWIFT. and the member banks concerned, appropriate procedures to handle incidents that may endanger the smooth functioning of the system and daily settlement

Certainty of daily settlement is ensured through the following features:

- The legal basis of the system provides a valid and enforceable single obligation or single claim of each participant towards the other banks in the system and vice versa. The Single Obligation Structure allows no unwind.

- The processing system is designed to ensure that no payment message is authorised for delivery if it would breach the sending participant's debit cap or the receiving participant's credit cap. A maximum debit cap and credit cap of EUR 1 billion is imposed on all banks.

- Payment messages that have been successfully processed are irrevocable and final within the system. Any return of funds is a matter which will be dealt with between the sending and the receiving participants and such return of funds via the EURO1 system necessitates the sending of a new payment message for an amount as will cancel the effects of the previously processed payment message.

- To ensure that settlement takes place in case one or several participants fail to cover their short positions in the system, a collateral pool of EUR 1 billion has been set up at the ECB.

Binding limits

Each participant has a debit cap and a credit cap in the system. The system ensures that the multilateral position resulting from the processing of a participant's payment messages (single obligation/single claim) never exceeds its debit or credit cap. Payment messages that would lead to a breach of the debit or credit cap are queued.

The discretionary element of the bilateral limits can only be changed until 18:00 on Day D-1. The limits cannot be changed or revoked until after settlement on that day. These limits are granted and adjusted by the participants according to their own risk management appetite.

Statistical data on the EURO1 system

	Average daily volume	Average daily value
January 2001	106,895	209 bio.
December 2000	112,537	216 bio.
November 2000	100,087	185 bio.
October 2000	98,839	188 bio.

APPENDIX 10

III

MAJOR ISO TRADING CURRENCY CODES

AUD	Australian dollars	MXN	Mexican Peso
BRL	Brazilian Real	MYR	Malaysian Ringgitts
CAD	Canadian Dollars	NOK	Norwegian Kroner
CHF	Swiss Francs	NTD	New Taiwanese Dollars
CZK	Czech Koruna	NZD	New Zealand Dollars
EEK	Estonian Kroon	PHP	Philippine Peso
EUR	Euro	PLN	Polish Zloty
GBP	Great Britain Pounds	RUB	Russian Rouble (New)
HKD	Hong Kong Dollars	RUR	Russian Rouble (old)
HUF	Hungarian Forint	SAR	Saudi Arabian Riyal
IDR	Indonesian Rupiah	SEK	Swedish Krona
INR	Indian Rupee	SKK	Slovak Koruna
ISK	Icelandic Krona	THB	Thai Baht
JPY	Japanese Yen	TRL	Turkish Lira
KRW	Korean Won (South)	TWD	New Taiwan Dollar
LVL	Latvian Lats	USD	US Dollars
		ZAR	South African Rand

APPENDIX 11

▌▌▌

FORMULAE

Money markets

The simple interest formula:

$$\frac{P \times R \times T}{100 \times Base}$$

where:
    I = Interest
    P = Principal
    R = Rate
    T = Time (number of days)

The discount formula:

$$\text{Proceeds} = FV - \left[FV\left(\frac{T \times DR}{B \times 100}\right)\right]$$

$$= 1{,}000{,}000 - \left[1{,}000{,}000\left(\frac{90 \times 10}{36500}\right)\right]$$

$$= 1{,}000{,}000 - 24{,}657.53 = 975{,}342.47$$

where:
    FV = Face Value
    T   = Time
    DR = Discount Rate
    B   = Base (360 or 365 days)

The true yield is:

$$\text{True yield} = \cfrac{\text{Discount rate}}{\left[1 - \left(\cfrac{\text{Discount rate x T}}{\text{Base x 100}}\right)\right]}$$

Formula for forward/forward or FRAs

The formula for forward/forward interest rate, or FRAs as is commonly known, is:

$$\left[\cfrac{\left(R_L \times D_L\right) - \left(R_s \times D_s\right)}{\left(D_L \times D_s\right) \times \left[1 + \cfrac{\left(R_s \times D_s\right)}{\left(B \times 100\right)}\right]}\right]$$

RL	=	Rate from start date to the far date (long period)
DL	=	Number of days from spot to the far date
RS	=	Rate from spot to the near date (short period)
DS	=	Number of days from spot to the near date
B	=	Day basis (360 or 365)

n.b. Some currencies are quoted from same day value, e.g. GBP.

The FRA settlement formula is:

$$\frac{(L - R) \text{ or } (R - L) \times D \times A}{(D \times L) + (B \times 100)}$$

L	=	Libor (BBA settlement rate)
R	=	Contract reference rate
A	=	Contract amount
D	=	Days in contract period
B	=	Day basis (360 or 365)

The present value over several periods

Present value $=$ $\dfrac{\text{Future value in Year 'n'}}{(1 + r)\, n}$

Where 'r' is interest/discount rate applying (expressed as a decimal - i.e. 10% = 0.10) and 'n' is the number of years. Therefore, if the discount rate is 10% and FV is £100 then today £100 is worth £100/1.10 = £90.91 : £100 FV in two years is £100/1.21 = £82.64, etc.

The semi-annual to annual rate of 6.86% must be annualised using the following conversion formula:

$$[(1+ \tfrac{6.86}{200})2\text{-}1] \times 100 = 6.9776$$

To convert the annual rate of 7.45% to a semi-annual equivalent use the following conversion formula:

$$\left[\sqrt{\dfrac{1+7.45}{100}} \right] 1 \times 200 = 7.3161$$

Options

Delta

The delta of an option measures the change in the price of an option relative to the change in the price of the underlying thus:

Delta $=$ $\dfrac{\text{change in price of option}}{\text{change in price of underlying}}$

Thus if USD/DEM changes from 1.82 to 1.78, an option price by 2 US cents, then the delta is expressed as 2/4 = 0.5.

Deltas can never change more than the change in the underlying, also the cost of the option cannot move in the opposite direction to the change in the underlying, thus the maximum range of delta is 0 to 1.

An option close to maturity which is in-the-money will thus have a delta which tends towards 1, while one that is out-of-the-money will tend towards zero.

Gamma

The gamma of an option measure the change in the delta compared to the change in the underlying and is expressed thus:

$$\text{Gamma} \quad = \quad \frac{\text{change in delta}}{\text{change in underlying}}$$

Thus, if delta for USD/DEM option moves from 0.5 to 0.6, and the underlying from 1.82 to 1.78, then gamma = 0.1/4 = 0.25.

Gamma is highest when the option is near to maturity and close to being at-the-money. Gamma tends to zero for deep in-the-money or deep out-of-the-money options.

Gamma is often used in constructing a position that would benefit from high volatility. This would be the purchase of a straddle where you buy a call and put at the same strike, so that - provided the option price does change enough in either direction - there will be a profit on either the call or the put which will exceed the loss on the other option which would be limited to the premium paid.

Theta

The theta of an option measures the change in the options price to the decrease in time to expiry. The value of an option decreases as time goes by - time decay - and thus the theta of an option has to be negative, so that an option with a theta of 0.025% would lose USD 250 per day on a nominal value of USD 1,000,000.

Theta is highest when options are at the money (ATM) and it is less susceptible to changes at the beginning of the period but decays rapidly towards expiry.

Vega or kappa

The vega monitors the change in the option's price relative to changes in volatility. Thus were volatility to increase 1% and the premium increased by USD 2,500, then the vega would be quoted as 0.25% on a face value of an option of USD 1,000,000.

Vega is highest when options are ATM and are a bigger influence on the price of the option the longer the maturity.

Rho

The rho measures the change in the price compared to the change in interest rates. Even if the spot price does not change, since the forward price is based on interest rate differentials, then a move in either interest rate will affect the price of the option. However, since we are only concerned with the difference between the two rates, rho is the least influential of factors in options pricing. Thus, if the differential moves by 1% and price by USD 1.25 then its rho is +1.25.

Calculating payment under cap

$$\frac{(\text{Libor - strike rate}) \times \text{days} \times \text{notional amount}}{\text{Days basis} \times 100}$$

Calculating payment on floor

$$\frac{(\text{Strike rate - Libor}) \times \text{days} \times \text{notional amount}}{\text{Days basis} \times 100}$$

APPENDIX 12

▌▌▌

CALENDAR BASIS

The alternative calendar conventions for calculating day count and annual basis are as follows:

Actual/actual: This means the day count is the actual number of days in the period. but the annual basis is the number of days in current coupon - multiplied by the number of coupons per annum, which means that coupon payments are always equal amounts.

Actual/365 (A/365): The annual basis is 365 days and the day count is the actual number of days in the period.

30E/360: The annual basis is 360 days and it is assumed that there is never more or less than 30 days in the day count for a complete month.

30/360: This is similar to the 30E/360 days in that there is assumed to be never more than 30 days in the day count for a month.

The difference between the 30E/360 and 30/360 convention can be shown by the following table:

Number of days of interest accrued from 1 July			
To	30 July	31 July	1 August
30E/360	29	29	30
30/360	29	30	30

Actual/360 (A/360): The annual basis is 360 days and the day count is the actual number of days in the period.

Actual/actual: The annual basis for semi-annual bonds is twice the actual number of days in the current semi-annual coupon period. The day count is the actual number of days in the period.

APPENDIX 13

III

OPERATIONAL RISK ACCORDING TO GENERALLY ACCEPTED REPORTING PROCEDURE (GARP)

Transaction risk

Execution error
Product complexity
Booking error
Settlement error
Commodity delivery risk
Documentary/contract risk

Operational control risk

Exceeding limit
Rogue trading
Deaud
Money laundering
Security risk
Key personnel risk
Processing risk

Systems risk

Programming error
Model/methodology error
Market-to-market error
Management information
IT systems failure
Telecommunications failure
Contingency planning

Business events risk

Currency convertability risk
Shift in credit rating
Reputation risk
Taxation risk
Legal risk
Disaster risk
Natural disasters
Wars
Collapse/suspension of market

Regulatory risk

Breaching capital requirements
Regulatory changes

APPENDIX 14

█ █ █

FUTURES CONTRACTS - EXAMPLES ON THE LONDON INTERNATIONAL FINANCIAL FUTURES EXCHANGE (LIFFE)

Futures

Short-term interest rate

Three-month sterling
Three-month Euroswiss
Three-month euro
Three-month Euroyen

Government bonds

Long gilt
Japanese government bond (JGB)

UK stock indices

FT-SE 100 (Financial Times Stock Exchange)
FT-SE mid-250

Options

Options on short-term interest rate futures

Three-month sterling
Three-month Euroswiss

Options on government bond futures

Long gilt

UK stock index options

FT-SE 100 (American-style exercise)
FT-SE 100 (European-style exercise)
FT-SE 100 FLEX

APPENDIX 15

III

MODEL OF CONDUCT -
SUMMARY OF CHAPTERS

APPENDIX 16

███

USEFUL ADDRESSES

APACS
Mercury House
Triton Court
14 Finsbury Square
London FC2A I BR
Tel: 020 7211 6200
www.apacs.org.uk

BACS Limited
3 De Havilland Road
Edgware
Middlesex HA8 SQA
Tel: 0870 0100699

CHAPS
(address as for APACS)
Tel: 020 7211 6200

The Bank of England
Policy/editorial
Threadneedle Street
London EC2R 8AH
Tel: 020 7601 4300

The Bank for International Settlements
Basel
Switzerland
Tel: + 4161 280 8080
Fax: + 4161 280 9100/8100
www.bis.org

Bloomberg LP
City Gate House
39-45 Finsbury Square
London EC2A 1PQ
Tel: 020 7330 7500
Fax: 020 7392 6200

The British Banker's Association
Pinners Hall
105-108 Old Broad Street
London EC2N lEX

The Building Societies Association
3 Savile Row
London W1X 1AF
Tel: 020 7437 0655

Clearstream Group
UK:
Floor 42
One Canada Square
Canary Wharf
London E14 5DR
Tel: 020 7682 7040/50
Europe:
67 Boulevard Grande
Duchesse Charlotte
L-1331
Luxembourg
Tel: +352 44 99 29081
Fax: +352 44 99 29 47 4
www.clearstreamgroup.com

CLS Bank
Exchange Tower
One Harbour Exchange Square
London E14 9GE
Tel: 020 7971 5700

Euroclear Bank
1, Boulevard du Roi Albert II
B-1210 Brussels
Belgium
Tel: +32 2 224 2618

Euronext/LIFFE
Cannon Bridge House
1, Cousin Lane
London EC4R 3XX
Tel: 020 7623 0444
Fax: 020 7588 3624

The Financial Services Authority
25, The North Colonnade
Canary Wharf
London E14 5HS
Tel: 020 7676 1000
Fax: 020 7676 1099

The Futures and Options Association
4th Floor
The Minories
London EC3N 1LS
Tel: 020 7426 7250
Fax: 020 7426 7251
info@foa.co.uk
www.foa.co.uk

International Petroleum Exchange
International House
1 St Katherine's Way
London E1W 1UY
Tel: 020 7481 0643
Fax: 020 7481 8485
www.ipe.uk.com

London Metal Exchange
56 Leadenhall Street
London EC3A 2DX
Tel: 020 7264 5522
Fax: 020 7690 0505
info@lme.co.uk

The London Clearing House Ltd
Aldgate House
33 Aldgate High Street
London EC3N 1EA
Tel: 020 7426 7042
Fax: 020 7426 7001

The London Stock Exchange
London EC2N 1HP
Tel: 020 7797 1000
Fax: 01959 561 721
www.londonstockexuser.co.uk

Reuters
Europe/UK:
Corporate Headquarters
Reuters Group plc
85 Fleet Street
London EC4P 4AJ
Tel: 020 7250 1122
America :
3, Times Square
New York
NY 10036
USA
Tel: +1 646 223 4000
Asia:
18 Science Park Drive
Singapore 119229
Republic of Singapore
Tel: +65 775 5088

SWIFT
Headquarters:
1 Avenue Adèle
B-1310 La Hulpe
Belgium
Tel: +32 2 655 3111
Fax: +32 2 655 3226

APPENDIX 17

▌▌▌

RELATIVE SIZE OF STOCK MARKETS

Relative Size of EU Stock Exchanges, Dec 2002

Country	Market Cap ($ mn)	Trading ($ mn)	Listed Companies
Austria	33,578	6,142	129
Denmark	76,750	53,101	201
Euronext*	1,538,654	1,987,199	1,492
Finland	138,833	178,596	149
Germany	686,014	1,207,977	934
Greece	67,062	23,512	314
Ireland	59,938	33,532	76
Italy	477,075	636,821	294
Luxembourg	24,551	491	244
Norway	64,170	56,058	204
Spain (BME)#	461,560	654,743	3,015
Sweden	179,117	277,495	297
U.K.	1,785,199	3,998,462	2,824

* Euronext includes Amsterdam, Brussels, Lisbon and Paris figures. Listed companies figures are Nov 2002, Dec not available.
# BME includes Barcelona, Bilbao, Madrid and Valencia figures.

Source: World Federation of Exchanges, 2002

Relative Size of Asian and Pacific Stock Exchanges, Dec 2002

Country	Market Cap ($ mn)	Trading ($ mn)	Listed Companies
Australian	380,087	295,649	1,421
Hong Kong	463,055	194,003	978
Indonesia	30,067	13,050	330
Malaysia	125,778	33,109	860
Philippines	18,507	3,107	235
Singapore	99,807	62,770	385
Taiwan	261,211	632,666	640
Thailand	45,504	41,292	398
Tokyo	2,069,299	1,565,824	2,153

Source: World Federation of Exchanges, 2002

U.S. Stock Exchanges, Dec 2002

Exchange	Market Cap ($ mn)	Trading ($ mn)	Listed Companies
NYSE	9,015,167	10,311,156	2,366
Amex	44,769	642,181	572
Nasdaq	1,994,494	7,254,595.3	3,649
Chicago	122	532,040	169
Toronto	573,403	406,041	1,304

Source: World Federation of Exchanges, 2002

APPENDIX 18

▌▌▌

SECURITY SETTLEMENT STATISTICS

Settlement volumes in selected securities settlement systems (daily average)

System	Location	Securities Type	Settlement volume US$bn 1994	Growth rate % 1988-94
Fedwire	USA	Government	578.8	7.9
JGB	Japan	Government	132.1	7.6
CGO	UK	Government	93.6	51.3
Euroclear	ICSD	Govt.; equities; other	84.7	40.5
DTC/SDFS	USA	Other	81.2	116.0
CDS/BBS	Canada	Govt.; equities; other	60.0	n.a.
DTC/NDFS	USA	Equities; other	52.8	8.9
RELIT	France	Govt.; equities; other	37.4	19.5
LDT	Italy	Govt.; equities; other	31.1	74.6
Cedel	ICSD	Govt.; equities; other	27.1	26.8
VPC	Sweden	Govt.; equities; other	24.4	n.a.
DKV	Germany	Govt.; equities; other	23.5	27.7
Saturne	France	Government; other	22.0	67.0
CMO	UK	Other	15.6	15.4
NBB	Belgium	Government; other	8.0	53.1
SEGA	Switz.	Govt.; equities; other	2.2	15.3
SCC	Netherl.	Govt.; equities; other	n.a.	n.a.

APPENDIX 19

███

ABBREVIATIONS
AND ACRONYMS

ABBL	-	Association of Banks and Bankers in Luxembourg
ABSAL	-	American Banking and Securities Association in London
AEX	-	Amsterdam Exchange
AITC	-	Association of Investment Trust Companies
APACS:	-	Association for Payment Clearing Services
ATM	-	Automated Teller Machine
AUTIF	-	Association of Unit Trusts and Investment Funds
BACS	-	Bulk Automated Clearing System
BAG	-	Business Advisory Group
BBA	-	British Bankers' Association
Bobi	-	Bundesobligationen
BOT	-	Buoni Ordinari del Tesoro
BTAN	-	Bons du Trésor à taux fixe et intérêts annuels
BTF	-	Bons du Trésor à taux fixe et intérêts précomptés
BTP	-	Buono del Tesoro Poliennali
CCBM	-	Correspondent Central Banking Model

CCT	-	Certificati di Crediti del Tesoro
CD	-	Certificate of Deposit
CET	-	Central European Time
CGO	-	Central Gilts Office
CHAPS	-	Clearing House Automated Payment System
CHIPS	-	Clearing House Interbank Payments System (New York)
CIK	-	Caisse Interprofessionelle de Dépôts et de Virements de Titres
CMO	-	Central Moneymarkets Office
CONSOB	-	Commissione Nazionale per la Società e la Borsa
CSDs	-	Central Securities Depositories
CTZ	-	Certificati del Tesoro (zero-coupon Italian bonds)
DBC	-	Deutsche Börse Clearing AG
DTB	-	Deutsche Terminbörse
DVP	-	Delivery-versus-Payment
EAF 2	-	Elektronische Abrechnung Frankfurt (net settlement system)
EBA	-	Euro Banking Association
ECB	-	European Central Bank
ECOFIN	-	Council of Finance and Economic Ministers of the European Union
ECSDA	-	European Central Securities Depositories Association
EFFAS	-	European Federation of Financial Analyst Societies
EMI	-	European Monetary Institute

EMS	-	European Monetary System
EONIA	-	Euro Overnight Index Average
ERM2	-	Exchange Rate Mechanism 2
ESCB	-	European System of Central Banks
ESDP	-	Exchange Delivery Settlement Plan
ETC	-	Electronic Trading Confirmation
FCCC	-	First Chicago Clearing Centre
FEE	-	Fédération des Experts Comptables Eurpéens
FIBOR	-	Frankfurt Interbank Offer Rate
FISD	-	Financial Information Services Division (Information Industry Association, IIA)
FLP	-	Financial Law Panel
FRNs	-	Floating Rate Notes
FSA	-	Financial Services Authority
FT/S&P-AWI		Financial Times/Standard and Poors' - Actuaries World Indices
FTSE	-	Financial Times Stock Exchange (indices)
ICAEW	-	Institute of Chartered Accountants in England and Wales
ICSDs	-	International Central Securities Depositories (Euroclear and Cedel)
IFMA	-	Institutional Fund Managers' Association
ILU	-	Institute of London Underwriters
IMF	-	International Monetary Fund
IMRO	-	Investment Management Regulatory Organisation
IPMA	-	International Primary Markets Association

ISDA	-	International Swaps and Derivatives Association
ISIN	-	International Securities Identification Number
ISMA	-	International Securities Markets Association
ISO	-	International Standards Organisation
ISTs	-	Inter-System Transfers
LIBA	-	London Investment Banking Association
LIBOR	-	London Interbank Offer Rate
LIFFE	-	London International Financial Futures and Options Exchange
LIRMA	-	London International Insurance and Reinsurance Market Association
LPC	-	London Processing Centre
LSE	-	London Stock Exchange
MATIF	-	Marché à Terme International de France
MFI	-	Monetary Financial Institution
MTNs	-	Medium-Term Notes
MTS	-	Mercato Telematico Secondario
NAPF	-	National Association of Pension Funds
NCB	-	National Central Bank
NCU	-	National Currency Unit
OAT	-	Obligations Assimilables du Trésor
OEICS	-	Open-ended investment companies
OLOS	-	Obligations Linéaires - lineaire oblligaties (Belgian government bond)
OLUX	-	Obligations Linéaires en Luxembourg Franc
OTC	-	Over-the-Counter

PIA	-	Personal Investment Authority
PIBOR	-	Paris Interbank Offer Rate
POS	-	Point of Sale
PSA	-	Public Scurities Association (New York)
RIBOR	-	Rome Interbank Offer Rate
RTGS	-	Real-Time Gross Settlement
SEDOL	-	Stock Exchange Daily Official List
SETS:	-	Stock Exchange Electronic Trading Service
SDRs	-	Special Drawing Rights
SFA	-	Securities and Futures Authority
SICOVAM		Société Interprofessionnelle pour la compensation des Valeurs Mobilères
SSIs	-	Standard Settlement Instructions
SSAPS	-	Statements of Standard Accounting Practice
STIR	-	Short-Term Interest Rate
SWIFT	-	Society for Worldwide Inter-bank Financial Telecommunications
TARGET	-	Trans-European Automated Real-time Gross settlement Express Transfer system
TCNs	-	Tires de Créances Négociables
UITF	-	Urget Issues Task Force
VAR	-	Value-at-Risk

▌▌▌

GLOSSARY OF TERMS

ACS
Automated confirmations system which includes BART and TRAM.

Arbitrage
Simultaneous purchase and sale of a currency in two or more markets to take advantage of discrepancies in prices. Spot forward or both. Often now used to mean 'interest arbitrage'.

Assignment of FX contract
A contract between one of the bank's customers and another bank on which you agree to accept your customer's responsibilities under the contract in return for a cash receipt/payment.

BART
Bank's automated reception terminal - i.e. the PC at which a bank accesses ACS, etc.

Bid
Price at which a price maker is willing to borrow or purchase a foreign currency.

BIS
The Bank for International Settlements, Basel. The Central Bank's central bank.

Broken dates
Rates quoted for specific dates between recognised dealing period - e.g. 1 month and 22 days, which lies between the straight one month and two month maturities.

Cable
The term given to spot GBP/USD, since originally the price went via a cable under the Atlantic.

CAD
The Capital Adequacy Directive of 1996 from BIS.

Call/demand
Short-term funds similar to current accounts which provide immediate funds and attract interest.

Cap
A cap is a loan where the rate is fixed at a maximum level at the outset and will not vary even if market rates go above the level of the cap. Also if the variable rate goes below the cap, the borrower will often get the benefit of a lower rate.

Clearstream
Clearstream is an institution which settles bonds, etc, on behalf of institutions (see Appendix 4).

Certificate of deposit (CD)
A negotiable certificate of deposit is a marketable receipt for funds deposited in a bank for a specified rate of interest. Domestic and euro CDs are issued on a 360-day basis with interest paid at maturity if the instrument has a maturity of one year or less (euro's annual if past one year). Since it is a tradeable security it is usually issued in bearer form.

CGO
Central Gilts Office,based at the Bank of England. This is an electronic settlement facility for gilts only (see also CMO).

CHAPS
A UK institution for the settlement of GBP payments (see Appendix 3).

CHIPS
A US based organisation which settles USD payments on behalf of correspondents (see Appendix 3).

CIRS
A currency interest rate swap where more than one currency is involved.

CMO
Central Money Markets Office, based at the Bank of England for all non-gilts GBP settlements (see also CGO).

Collar
A collar sets an upper and lower base for the interest rate on a loan/investment.

Collateral deposit
A deposit taken as security for a loan, or cover of a letter of credit. It could be either fixed or at call.

Convertibility
A currency can be exchanged for another currency without restrictions irrespective of who owns the money and without having to obtain permission from the authorities.

Cross rate
Normal interpretation is an exchange of one foreign currency for another, other than local currency - i.e. in New York, any pair of currencies which does not include USD, e.g. EUR/JPY.

Customer daily settlement limit
The maximum cumulative amount in all currencies spot and/or future, to be settled on any single day by a customer. One side only of each transaction shall be included in this calculation.

Customer foreign exchange limit
The maximum cumulative amount (often now the net amount) of dealings spot and/or forward, in any or all currencies that is permitted to be outstanding at any one time in the name of a customer. One side only of each transaction shall be included in this calculation.

Dealing date
The date on which a deal is actually contracted.

Discount
When currency A buys less of currency B at a future date then A is said to be at a discount to B.

EBS
European Broking System - a rival electronic broking system to R-2002.

ECB

The ECB is the new European Central Bank based in Frankfurt which will set policy and rates for all the 11 members of the euro.

Federal funds

Purchase or sale of uncommitted Fed member bank deposits, usually overnight, at a specified Fed funds rate.

Fixed deposit

A deposit taken for a fixed period of time at a fixed rate of interest. Fixed deposits may be repaid prior to maturity but are subject to an interest adjustment based on the cost of replacing the funds to the maturity of the deposit.

Floor

A floor is a guaranteed minimum rate of return on a deposit. Thus the depositor will receive the rate on the floor even if market rates go below its level.

Foreign currency loan

A loan denominated in non-local currencies, which is extended by a bank to a correspondent.

Foreign exchange gap

Gaps are created by mismatched maturities in each currency's forward exchange book. These gaps represent foreign exchange risk.

Foreign exchange swap

The simultaneous purchase (or sale) of an amount of foreign currency against the sale (or purchase) of the same amount of currency for a different date. The following three definitions are special cases of swaps, all related to funding, and distinguished by their purpose:

- *Position swap:* The execution of a foreign exchange swap to close a net foreign exchange position which resulted from making loan and placements and accepting deposits in a variety of currencies without attempting to exactly match.

- *Funding swap general:* The execution of a foreign exchange swap to generate funds in a currency for which there is an anticipated need from funds in a currency which is available or a currency which, together with a swap premium/discount, is attractively priced.

• *Funding swap specific:* The execution of a foreign exchange swap to generate currency to fund a specific asset from deposit funds in another currency and to sell the loan proceeds forward for the deposit currency.

Foreign exchange trading

The process of trading a given amount of one national currency for the approximate equivalent value of another currency. Currencies are usually traded with correspondents in spot trades, outright forward trades or swaps.

Forward

A forward contract is a foreign exchange deal made for delivery on any value date in the future. For practical purposes it is defined as a purchase or sale of foreign currencies against sterling or another currency for commercial purposes or cover of principal and interest on foreign currency loans and deposits, to mature at a given date normally over and above seven days. A forward contract is entered into to eliminate any risk of exchange rates moving between the time that a commitment is first established and the date of actual delivery of funds. For example, if one of the bank's customers knows that in three months time it will need dollars for payment of goods imported from the USA it will buy these dollars from the bank now on a forward basis, value date on which the import is required to be settled. This eliminates any risk of rate movements between now and three month's time, and since the customer knows now what the exchange is it can calculate its costs accordingly. The dealer in turn would normally cover the deal in the market.

Option exchange contract

A contract for foreign exchange with an optional settlement date. In this type of contract, a period of time is stated during which the person who has the option can choose any day for liquidation and settlement of the contract. The contract will state which party has the option and is usually employed when the date on which foreign exchange will be needed or will be available is not known. These options must be carried out by the final date of the contract.

FRA

An FRA is defined as a forward rate agreement between any two banks seeking to protect themselves against a future interest movement in interest rates. The two parties involved agree an interest rate for a specified period of time, from a specified future settlement date (minimum period one month) based on an agreed principal amount.

FSA
The Financial Services Authority is the regulatory body in the UK which now assumes responsibility for control of all markets in the UK - FX, MM, insurance etc.

Funding gap
Gaps created by mismatched maturities in each individual currency's asset and liability portfolio. These gaps represent interest rate risk.

Futures
These represent a firm commitment to buy or sell a specific commodity, during a specified month at a price established through open auction or outcry in a central regulated market place.

Hedging
Hedging is carried out to reduce risk on known future exposures whether in the FX or money markets.

IRS
An IRS is an interest rate swap - a means of changing the interest flows from fixed to floating or vice versa.

Libor
London Inter Bank Offered Rate. Each day at 11 am a group of bankers declare their offered rates for the traditional fixed periods, - i.e. 1, 2, 3 or 6 months. The mean rate is thus established as the Libor fixing or basis for all commercial loan agreements and FRABBA terms (see Appendix 2) for off-balance sheet trading instruments.

LIFFE
The London International Financial Futures Exchange - it was an all 'open outcry' market for the trading of financial futures and options but is now heavily mechanised to screen trading.

Line of credit
An obligation to extend short-term credit to a correspondent, subject to periodic review, amendment or cancellation at any time.

Long
Long in a currency means overbought spot, forward or in total.

MLRO
A money laundering reporting officer, who is required, under Bank of England requirements, to report any suspicion that the source of funds may be from illegal sources, e.g. drugs.

Money market investments
These provide correspondents with ways to cover their temporary cash surpluses into short-term earnings assets through highly liquid instruments.

NCB
An NCB is the term applied to the National Central Bank of a member country of the euro as opposed to the ECB or European Central Bank.

NDFs
Non-deliverable forwards - a system for trading in exotic currencies where forwards would normally be restricted or unavailable.

Nostro
Your nostro account is an account in a foreign currency where you take delivery of that currency.

Off-balance sheet items
These instruments, unlike cash, do not cause money to change hands upon their purchase or sale and therefore do not represent assets when owned. They are contingent liabilities which bind the owner to some future action.

Offer
The rate at which a price maker is willing to either lend or sell a foreign currency.

Options
A buyer is granted the right (but not the obligation) to buy or sell financial instruments at standard prices and times in the future.

Outright
Merely the second half of a swap, but made up of the spot rate plus or minus the forward points.

Overdraft loan
Short-term loan extended by the bank to a correspondent to fulfil unexpected funding requirements.

Pips
A pip or point in a foreign exchange quotation is literally the last digit in the quotation (normally the fourth place to right of decimal). If one sterling GBP equals 1.5501 USD, then one pip is 0.0001 of a dollar.

Premium
When currency A buys more of currency B at a future date then A is said to be at a premium to B.

Prime rate
The minimum interest rate that banks charge their biggest, best and most creditworthy corporate customers. It is a base on which to scale all interest rates.

Repurchase agreements
Contracts involving the sale of government and agency securities with commitment to repurchase at a future date at the same price plus a stipulated interest charge. The USA had the first market, but repurchase agreements now exist in most developed bond markets (Germany, UK, France, Italy, etc). There are two types - 'sell/buy back' and 'classic'. Settlements for both are described in detail in Appendix 6.

Reverse repurchase agreements
Contracts involving the purchase of securities with commitment to return them at a future date for the original price plus interest.

Revolving credit
A formal commitment allowing a correspondent to borrow and repay loans at will under specific terms and conditions.

Rollover
Banks are typically borrowers of short-term funds but lenders of long-term funds, consequently they are vulnerable to upward movements in interest rates which would increase the cost of their own borrowings but not necessarily that of their loans. Therefore they vary terms of their loans at regular intervals to reflect changes in the cost of funds.

RTGS
Real time gross settlement is the name given to the most recent 'system' to ensure 'finality of payment', i.e. a system that will ensure that both parties receive simultaneously the amounts due to them, thereby guaranteeing that a Herstatt situation cannot arise.

Short
Short in a currency means oversold spot, forward or in total.

Spot
The purchase or sale of foreign currencies which normally must be received or delivered within a period of time not exceeding two business days. Occasionally, purchases or sales of foreign currencies are made for delivery three and five business days after the dealing date, to allow for weekends and/or holidays. Some countries practice delivery after three to five days anyway and still call this 'spot'.

Spread
The point/interest rate difference between the bid and offer price.

SRO
Self-regulating organisation, e.g. LAUTRO for life assurance. All SROs have come together under the Financial Services Authority (FSA).

SSIs
Standard settlement instructions which are exchanged between counterparts to specify the agent (nostro) where they will always take delivery of a specific currency.

Swap cost and swap income
In funding swap transactions, the differences between the spot and forward rates is regarded as an interest factor called the swap cost or swap income.

SWIFT
Society for Worldwide International Financial Telecommunications, the prime agent in Europe for the settlement of foreign currency transactions.

TARGET
The name of the settlement system for the euro.

Term loan
The formal commitment with a final maturity usually in excess of one year, in which a correspondent repays according to a formal agreement.

TRAM
Transaction automatic matching - part of the ACS - for the automatic matching of confirmations.

TRAX
The system into which all bond transactions have to be entered within 30 minutes of execution to allow confirmation to take place.

Triangulation
The term given to the method of working out the countervalue of two 'in' currencies against each other via their rates against the euro.

Value date
The date on which the transaction is to be settled (delivery or receipt of funds).

VaR
Value at risk, the most recent development in assessing the market risk of an institution's complete exposure. The three main methods are covariance, historical and Monte Carlo.

Vostro
A vostro account is the account held by another bank at your bank, e.g. GBP account held by Deutsche Bank with your bank in London.

Yard
A slang term for 1,000 million (an American billion) of a currency. Now only usually used for JPY.

▌▌▌

SOFTWARE
COMPANY DETAILS

ACT Financial Systems

• Supports forex trading in the domestic, international and emerging markets.
• RIMS provides processing environment across multiple markets in all currencies.
www.actfs.co.uk

AVT Technologies

• Provides financial institutions on a private label basis.
• EchoFX enables real-time, electronic forex dealing in spot, forwards and swaps.
www.avt.co.uk

Cognotec

• Provides bank-branded, web-based pricing and trade execution services for forex and money market dealing.
www.cognotec.com

CSK Software

• Supplies middleware, internet, trading floor, retail banking and data distribution technology.
• Addresses requirements from price quotation, trade routing and execution to final settlement.
www.csksoftware.com

Dene / International Financial Systems

• Provides platform for banks to offer branded electronic trading.
• Can restrict users to certain instruments, currencies or markets.
www.ifs.ie

digitec

• d3 family of products available for forex and money market trading.
www.digitec.de

eSpeed

• eSpeed builds and operates global, interactive and business-to-business electronic markets.
• eSpeedSM system enables market participants to transact business instantly.
www.espeed.com

Fenics

• Analytics with online forex options trading.
www.fenics.com

Financial Market Solutions

• Fully automated Web-based platform to simultaneously access the system and execute forex trades.
www.fms2000.com

Financial Objects

• Financial services provided by ActiveBank system.
www.finobj.com

Financial Software Systems

• Spectrum product provides front, middle- and back-office system for forex and interest rate dealers.
www.fssnet.com

FNX

• Trading workflow management and accounting system.
www.fnx.com

Integral

• Products provide banks with time-to-market advantages, lower risk, lower costs.
www.integral.com

Madge.web

• Applications and managed network services.
• Uses own Overnet system for secure data network services for the financial markets.
www.madgeweb.com

Midas Kapiti International

• Provides back-office, universal and wholesale banking solutions.
www.midas-kapiti.com

Midlandeuro

• Forex-trading software for solid stable online trading platforms.
www.midlandeuro.com

Oxford Global Network

• Provides online real-time dealing / trading solutions.
• Customer and dealing desk interfaces and back-office functionality.
www.fx3000.com

patsystems

• Provides trading and risk management for multiple futures, options and cash equity exchanges.
• Integrated order routing, risk management and user administration software.
www.patsystems.com

Pixelpark

• Provides strategic consulting, design implementation, technical integration and the handling of logistics for e-commerce banking.
www.pixelpark.com

Reuters

• Provides own-branded, internet trading services for corporate and institutional customers.
• Modular solutions for STP and messaging software.
www.about.reuters.com

Shadow Financial Services

• Provides modules to support forex, metals, global sovereign debt, equities, futures, options, OTC options and swaps.
www.shadowfinancial.com

Summit Systems

• High volume trading with real-time position-keeping etc.
www.summithq.com

SunGard Trading and Risk Systems

• Solutions for trading, risk management and operations, asset liability management and financial planning and forecasting.
www.risk.sungard.com

Trema

• Offers technology solutions and consulting services.
www.trema.com

Velocity Systems

• Offers rate engine, integrated credit and margin / profile management.
www.velsys.com

Zero Base Development

• Products for forex markets.
www.zerobase.com

BIBLIOGRAPHY

General

The Foreign Exchange and Money Markets Guide
by Julian Walmsley,
Wiley, 2nd Edition, 2000

Derivatives - general

An Introduction to Derivatives
from Reuters Ltd,
Wiley, 1st Edition, 1999

Mastering Derivatives Markets
by Francesca Taylor,
FT Pitman, 2nd Edition, 2000

EMU and the euro

Practical Issues Arising from the Introduction of the Euro
periodically issued free by the Bank of England,
(available at: www.bankofengland.co.uk)

Futures

Futures, Options, and Swaps
by Robert Kolb,
Blackwell Publishers, 4th Edition, 2002

An Introduction, LIFFE
free from LIFFE,
(available at: www.liffe.com)

Options, Futures, and Other Derivatives
by John C. Hull
FT Prentice Hall (Higher Ed.), 5th Edition, 2002

The Futures Game
by Richard Teweles and Ben Warwick,
McGraw-Hill Professional, 3rd Edition 1999

Gilts

The Market in Gilt-Edged Securities and Annual Reviews
free from the Bank of England.
(available at: www.bankofengland.co.uk)

Handbook of Fixed Income Securities
by Frank J. Fabozzi,
McGraw-Hill Professional, 6th Edition, 2000

Introduction to Bond Markets
by Moorad Choudhry,
Securities Institute Services, 2nd Edition, 2001

An Introduction To Bond Markets
from Reuters Ltd,
Wiley, 1st Edition, 1999

Money Markets

An Introduction to Foreign Exchange and Money Markets
from Reuters Ltd,
Wiley, 1st Edition, 1999

The Money Market
by Marcia Stigum,
Dow Jones-Irwin, 3rd edition, 1990

Money Market and Bond Calculations
by Marcia Stigum,
Dow Jones-Irwin, 1st Edition, 1996

The Bond and Money Markets: Strategy, Trading, Analysis
by Moorad Choudhry,
Butterworth Heinemann, 1st Edition, 2001

Options

Foreign Exchange Options
by Alan Hicks,
Woodhead Publishing, 2nd Edition, 1998

Mastering Foreign Exchange and Currency Options
by Francesca Taylor,
FT Pitman, 1997 (New edition June 2003)

Regulations

London Code of Conduct
free from the Bank of England,
(available at: www.bankofengland.co.uk)

The Model Code
available from ACI Press

Financial Services Authority: The Handbook of Rules and Guidance
from The Financial Services Authority, Jan 2003,
(available at: www.fsa.gov.uk)

Repo

An Introduction to Repo Markets
by Moorad Choudhry,
Securities Institute Services, 1st Edition, 1999

REPO the Ultimate Guide
by Daniel Corrigan, Christopher Georgiou and Jonathan Gollow
Pearls of Wisdom Press, 1st Edition, 1999

Mastering Repo Markets
by Robert Steiner,
FT Pitman, 1st Edition, 1997

The Repo Handbook
by Moorad Choudhry,
Butterworth Heinemann, 1st Edition, 2002

Risks (derivatives)

Risk Management Guidelines for Derivatives
free from the Bank for International Settlements (BIS), July 1994
(available at: www.bis.org)

Analysing Sumitomo
by Mari Kooi,
published in Swiss Commodities, 1996,
(available at: www.riskinstitute.ch)

Not Just One Man
by Lilian Chew,
(available at: www.riskinstitute.ch)

When Genius Failed: the Rise and Fall of Long-Term Capital
Management
by Roger Lowenstein,
Fourth Estate, 1st Edition, 2002

Barings Bankruptcy and Financial Derivatives
by Peter Zhang,
World Scientific, 1995

Risk - operational
Report of the Board of Banking Supervision Inquiry into the collapse of
Barings
from the Bank of England, 1995,
(available at: www.bankofengland.co.uk)

268

The Year 2000: A Challenge for Financial Institutions and Bank Supervisors
Basel Committee on Banking Supervision, 1997.

Financial Institutions Reform, Recovery and Enforcement Act (FIRREA), 1989.

Report on Netting Schemes (The Angell Report)
free from the Bank for International Settlements (BIS) 1989,
(available at: www.bis.org)

Consultative paper on on-balance sheet netting
free from the Bank for International Settlements (BIS) 1998,
(available at: www.bis.org)

The Lamfalussy Standards
free from the Bank for International Settlements (BIS) 1990.
(available at: www.bis.org)

Real Time Gross Settlement - report Basel 1997
free from the Bank for International Settlements (BIS),
(available at: www.bis.org)

Risk (systemic)

Global Institutions, National Supervision and Systemic Risk
G-30 publication, 1997,
(available at: www.group3.org)

Risk (VaR)

Value at Risk
by Philippe Jorion,
Irwin,2nd Edition, 2000

Understanding and Applying Value at Risk
from Risk Publications,
Risk Books, 1st Edition 1997

An Introduction to Value at Risk
by Moorad Choudhry,
Securities Institute Services, 2nd Edition, 2001

Mastering Value at Risk
by Cormac Butler,
FT Prentice Hall

Swaps

An Introduction to Swaps
by Petros Geroulanos,
Securities Institute Services. 1st Edition 1999

Futures, Options, and Swaps
by Robert Kolb,
Blackwell Publishers, 4th Edition, 2002

Swaps and Other Derivatives
by Richard Flavell,
Wiley, 2002

Interest Rate Swaps
by Brian Coyle,
Financial World Publishing, 2001

Currency Swaps
by Financial World Publishing, 2000

Technical Analysis

Technical Analysis from A to Z
by Steven Achelis,
Probus, 2nd Edition, 2000

Technical Analysis of Stock Trends
by Robert Edwards and John Magee,
Amacom, 8th Edition 2001

Technical Analysis Explained
by Martin Pring,
McGraw-Hill Professional, 4th Edition 2002

Technical Analysis Applications in the Global Currency Markets
by Cornelius Luca,
NYIF, 2nd Edition, 2000

An Introduction to Technical Analysis
from Reuters Ltd,
Wiley, 1st Edition, 1999

Technical Analysis of the Financial Markets
by John J. Murphy,
New York Institute of Finance, 2nd Edition, 1999

III

INDEX